"*ACTION!*"
John 'Bud' Cardos

by Bob and Lynette Dix

Introduction by Gary Warner Kent

"ACTION!" John 'Bud' Cardos
by Bob and Lynette Dix

L & B Publishing
Copyright © 2016
First Edition 2016

10 9 8 7 6 5 4 3 2 1
ISBN-10: 0982243634
ISBN-13: 978-0-9822436-3-3

L & B Publishing
1030 S. Barrel Cactus Ridge
Benson, AZ 85602
www.RobertWDix.com

Printed in the United States of America

DEDICATION

I know my dedication of this book about my life is different, but I know animal lovers all over the world will understand.

I dedicate it to all my beloved animals — my pets here and gone on:

Horses:
- Trouble
- Double Trouble
- DT
- Fuego'
- Dusty
- Quincy Blue
- Spinner

Mule:
- Ludie Mae

Dogs:
- Trixie
- Pal
- Jonathan Benjamin Beam — Jim Beam
- Baron
- Caesar
- Samantha 'Sam'
- Rusty
- Russia
- K-Bar
- JR

Ape:
- Freddy Cardos

Lioness:
- Diane

Raccoon:
- Jimmy

Buffalo:
- Buffy

And to my partner in our Wild Sage Canyon Ranch, 'Letty' Guttilla, who will always be near and dear to my heart.

Contents

ACKNOWLEDGMENTS

The good Lord has been good to me allowing me a long life. In this book you will obtain a clear picture of a man who has been blessed with the breath of life far beyond just being lucky. I have "beat the odds."

The adventure of living has allowed me to meet, work with, and love many people along the way, some for a short time and some for many years. I am a true believer in the belief that true love never dies and when a man reaches my age closer to the end of life, my love for friends and family both here and beyond has never died. Each and every one of you I have known and loved are near and dear to my heart; including my five children, each in a special way. Judy and Cindy from my first marriage to Barbara; Debbie, Kimberly and John from my marriage to Pat; and my grandchildren and great-grandchildren: Ariel, Ashley, Linsey, Ryley, Autumn, Joshua, Jeremy, Haley, Brianna, Jonathan, Stacy, Justin, Brittany, Katrina, Natalie, Ryan, Danny, and Richard. The good times and the bad, the ups and downs of life together, has held a different and special love for each and will always be there even after I have left this life.

The same goes for my friends in the movie business. The movie stars, producers and crews, at many different levels, and people I have met all over the world, some still this side of the grass! To mention each one of you would create a small volume in itself. You know who you are and the special times we shared, often at:

Moose Lodge # 1738	Elks Lodge #2790
Reseda, CA	Van Nuys/Reseda, CA

Here are a few of crew member friends from the time shared working together in TV and movies:

Producer Emily Shelton	Tony and Javier Jimenez	Baker Boys
Kenny Kaplan	JT	Collin Butrum
Gerry Knight	Jim Herbert	Noah Ford
Tom Calzia	Mike Balew	Damion (Australian)
Mark Basher	Robert Leo's	Steve SHOE Shoemaker

To the hundreds not mentioned, the movie and television stars, cowboys, horse wranglers, special effects, stuntmen and all you guys and gals in editing rooms, music men and women and your collective talent that made the impossible possible: Thanks!

And my love always

– Cowboy Bud

An Introduction by Gary Warner Kent

"John 'Bud' Cardos. Sounds like a rodeo cowboy, doesn't it? One of those dusty drinks of water who comes riding out of the chute on the back of some two-ton beast frothing at the mouth, bent on throwing him into the muck and stomping the shit out of him." The voice belonged to famed movie director Quentin Tarantino, in town for his annual "QFest." We were seated at a table in the café of the San Juan hotel, in Austin, Texas, talking film, filmmakers, actors and stuntmen. "And now, outta' chute number seven comes that good-lookin' bull rider John 'Bud' Cardos, on top of ol' Hell to Pay, a bull that has never, ever been rode!!!"

Tarantino and I had just come from a screening of The Savage Seven, where he had just told a sold out audience that Chuck Bail, I and Bud Cardos were three of his favorite stuntmen, especially Bud, because of that cowboy sounding name. Bud, Chuck and I had major roles in the film, as well as doing most of the stunts, fights, bike-jumps, and raising hell in general. The three of us have all remained friends and working compatriots for over thirty-five years.

I first met Bud Cardos on a picture called Run Home Slow, starring Oscar winner Mercedes McCambridge and Linda Gaye Scott, heiress to the Scott Paper Company. I was co-starring as Ritt Hagen, Mercedes' Brother, who spends much of the film slumped over the back of a bony, cantankerous donkey, having been severely wounded in a gunfight. The cowpoke doing the wounding was a tall, dark-haired actor named John Bud Cardos. Bud, as he was called by most close friends, was also serving as stunt-coordinator, Production Manager, and head horse wrangler. A gentleman, I soon learned, of many talents and remarkable abilities.

Bud and I both loved movies, acting, doing stunts, even doing some of the heavy lifting required to get "it" all in the can, such as electrical, special effects and other crew work. We also discovered that we lived just a couple of blocks from each other, near the neighborhood of Coldwater and Moorpark in North Hollywood. It was a Los Angeles bedroom community shoved up against the Hollywood Hills on one side and spilling into the great San Fernando Valley on the other. Bud and I lived in shouting distance of each other, we both had families, a wife, kids, dogs, cats, the usual...only Bud also had lizards, scorpions, snakes and a monkey and cougar. Once in a while he would barbeque, and half the neighborhood would show up for the free food and beer. My place was a bit more barren than Bud's...he still jokes about attending a formal dinner I threw in which the main meal was served on a card table — with apple boxes for chairs.

Being neighbors and friends, and given our mutual love of horses, Bud and I just naturally bonded. On weekends we would pile into a car and boogie down to Compton to Tom Cloud's horse hangout. Cloud was a lanky, affable half-breed, half Cherokee, half African American, who had some of the meanest and mangiest animals in the county. From time to time, Cloud would rent them out as background stock to the studios, and also, on weekends, throw these little pumpkin-roller rodeos for the wranglers and out of work cowboys from the valley. Cardos and I would throw a few bucks into the hat and take our chances in bronc riding, bull dogging, ribbon roping ....winner take all. Frequently, at the end of the day, Bud was the one with the most points, the one who still had most of his bones in place, and the one who had somehow maintained the ability to walk straight.

The large expanse of Bud's personal warmth and popularity was made even more evident to me when we took his Cessna 182 on a hopscotch tour around the southwest, scouting locations for his close friend, the prodigious TV and Movie Producer Dick Clark. The trip included stops in Death Valley, Big Bear, Tucson, and Las Vegas. At every touchdown, we were met by old pals of Bud's, anxious to reconnect, buy us dinner, chat away the night recalling old times and fond memories. It quickly became obvious that wherever we landed, Bud had been there before; leaving behind a host of folks that absolutely adored him, considering themselves his best ever "pals." These happy reconnections continued non-stop throughout the entire flight. It says much about a man to have that amount of friends who have remained loyal Bud Cardos fans in spite of the rigors of distance and time.

This was a magical, wondrous era, the 60s and early 70s. It was a great time to be young, alive, and to be working in motion pictures. The Independent Film Revolution had burst on the scene with all of the gusto and bravado of a wedding crasher. The Drive-ins, Art Theaters and Grindhouses were all thirsting for product. Exploitation and low-budget filmmakers were having a field day. Bud and I jumped right into that dizzying dance, fluffed up and ready to rumble. Over the next forty years, we never left the dance floor.

So then, be it known that I worked with Mr. Cardos on a number of films over those halcyon, slap-happy, sometimes heart-breaking years. It was during the infancy of these creative times that Bud called me to work on a Biker/Nazi/Gangland opus titled Hell's Bloody Devils. The picture was helmed by the indefatigable and prolific director, Al Adamson. Adamson was known for making a host of gnarly, funky, highly entertaining movies, many of which continue to pop up to this day on TV and at festivals and retro-conventions world-wide. In 1969 Bud and I worked together for Adamson on Satan's Sadists, a raunchy, ultra-violent biker flick. Some Grindhouse fans consider Satan's to be the quintessential motorcycle movie of all time.

Besides a host of younger players, the cast included several popular actors that had starred in films for many years, including Scott Brady, Kent Taylor, and everyone's favorite acrobatic dancer, Russ Tamblyn. The film also starred tall, good looking Robert "Bob" Dix, son of famed movie actor Richard Dix. Bob and Bud were good friends, and it didn't take long before the three of us, sequestered for several weeks out on the fringe of the great Mojave Desert, and began to hang together in the off hours, singing, drinking, raising hell, and consuming mouthfuls of Bud's homemade rattlesnake pate. In Satan's Sadists, I was the good guy for once, while Cardos and Dix stayed true to form as two of the most fearsome and twisted cycle-jocks this side of Hollister. Talk about your Wild Ones!

It is Bob Dix, then, who has penned this superb biography of his lifetime friend, John Bud Cardos. Throughout the following pages, Dix will take you on an awesome, edgy and always entertaining tour through the life and times of John Bud Cardos, including interviews and sit-down-jaw-jacks with the man himself. The stories are all true, and over the course of several years, Bud has told Bob most of the ones that made it past the censors, and even some that didn't. All of the tales are colorful, and oft times hair-raising. As director Quentin Tarantino would say, "Now, out of chute #7'" comes John 'Bud' Cardos..."

So, bring in the dog, lock the doors and windows, grab a cup of coffee or pour yourself a glass of your favorite night-time cocktail, be it beer, wine, or like Bud, a glass of Jim Beam whiskey with just a whisper of water. Slip on your slippers, ease into the easy chair, turn the first page, and prepare yourself for one hell of a journey. Trust me; you are going to enjoy the ride.

Gary Warner Kent

Chapter One
Cowboy 'Bud' Cardos

"There ain't a cowboy who can't be throw'd and there ain't a horse that can't be rode!" To John 'Bud' Cardos, that well-known saying became his main motivation all of his life. It was in-born. It was "in his blood." There was never a problem that could not be solved, one way or another. A new approach was needed or more time to conquer the quest. Like a cowboy having been throw'd, dusts himself off and jumps back in the saddle. There are no guarantees in life but the horse learns it is best to let the cowboy ride.

Born in St. Louis, MO, December 20, 1928, to John Cardos, Sr. and his mother, Margaret, Bud got tagged with "junior" until some years of becoming his own person, friends and family needing a distinct line between father and son, 'Bud' became his name. He always admired and loved his father and mother and always honored them as a loving son.

Professional family portrait circa 1931–32

Bud brought his mother into his home and cared for her the last years of her life. A portrait of John Sr. hangs over the fireplace in the Cardos home today. John Sr. was a good father and teacher and a highly respected business man who taught by example.

When Bud was just a couple of years old, John Sr. decided to take his family west to California. The early 1930's cross-country roads were not always paved and often followed wagon trails pioneered by earlier Americans. Bouncing along with his sister, Christine, Dad and Mom and their family dog riding the running board of an old, Gardener Touring Car, the Cardos family moved west to San Gabriel, California, a community on the outskirts of Los Angeles.

Mom, Dad and Gardener touring car

Christine
Age 7½

John
Age 4½

CARDOS

"Mating Time"—Salient Prod.
"The Cracked Iceman"—Chase Comedy—Roach

GRanite 3601   **GLadstone 1109**

Being a Catholic family, Bud and his sister were enrolled in the local San Gabriel Mission School. When John Sr. got the job of managing the Egyptian Theater on Hollywood Blvd, Bud got his first break into Show Business. At about age four, the producers of "Our Gang" comedies cast Bud as one of the "Ruffians" for the movie series. Being athletic and a natural talent, he also learned how to sing and dance. At about age 6, with his straw hat, cane and a little tuxedo, Bud would tap, spin, sing and dance, entertaining audiences between movies not only for his father at the Egyptian but for the other theaters on Hollywood Blvd.

Dancing Bud Cardos

Watching movies, Bud was fascinated with the stunts performed by the Hollywood Stuntmen. He would try to recreate them in the backyard of their San Gabriel home. One time trying to recreate a fire stunt, he put his cousin in a wagon and rode with her in the wagon steering it through a ring of fire he built from wire and newspapers. The warmest part of the stunt was Bud's butt compliments of John Sr.

Bud at about six years old enjoyed showing off for the other kids, mainly the girls. One of his eye-catching stunts was to hang upside down from the top bar of the swing-set on the playground to eat his lunch. One day he lost his grip and fell on his head. He cracked his skull. Now he laughs saying, "Maybe that is why people have said to me, "Bud you are crazy! That stunt could have killed you!" To this day he is hard of hearing in his right ear from that early stunt.

Bud did different types of work including mowing lawns, and working at the local ice-cream parlor but the most rewarding employment was learning how to cook at his Dad's newly acquired restaurant in downtown Los Angeles, a profession that would serve him well later in life. "The bar on Spring Street in downtown L.A. was 100 feet long and the bartenders were on roller skates. One bartender was a "little person." It was quite a sight to see just the top of his head and a beer sailing the length of the bar to serve a customer," Bud recalls laughing.

During the High School years, track was Bud's favorite sport. The high-jump was the best event for him. He worked at it until at one Track Meet he cleared six-feet four inches, a school record that held for twelve years. Being a small school, if one of the athletes became injured or sick, Bud would fill in. Although he was not a pole-vault contender, the coach would call on him to do his best. Another sign of the Bud just being Bud, he would run at the high cross bar, insert the pole in the catch hole and, like a monkey, shimmy himself up the pole and throw his body over the cross-bar. The object was to get over the cross-bar any way possible creating this very unorthodox Cardos' method. "After all the idea was to get over the cross-bar so I did. It worked for me." Just another clue to Bud's later success in life in the Motion Picture Industry. Some methods may have been unorthodox but if they achieve the objective it was the result that counted.

Bud and fellow track members

Bud's social life was accented by a teenage affection for one particular girl, Joyce. It was more than puppy love, but boys and girls were very different in that day. The guys were athletic and generally shy. Girls were still heavily influenced by the Victorian standards of dating and told they must wait for marriage before total submission to their desires. Bud and Joyce did their share of youthful passion but stayed in the bounds of the rules promoted by their parents, not always easy. We all remember our own youth and its challenges.

One of the main reasons for Bud's respect for Joyce was because of her dad. He was a cop. It wasn't fear that kept young Cardos in the good graces of Paul, but a genuine friendship that developed between Bud and Paul, the cop who happened to be Joyce's father. He approved of and enjoyed the relationship between the teenagers.

One Halloween a neighbor to Paul's residence, who was known by the kids as "the Grouch," had bought a load of cement blocks to build a wall on his property line to further isolate him from the world. Bud and his buddy, John, waited until the lights in the Grouch's house went dark. After about an hour, they quietly parked Bud's car a house away from "The Grouch House." Quietly they proceeded to build a wall across the street in front of his house with the cement blocks 2 feet tall. Suddenly the lights went on. The guys raced to the car and returned to Paul's house several houses up the street.

Sitting on Paul's porch they saw the cops arrive and the Grouch protesting. The two cops proceeded to move the cement blocks back onto Grouch's property. The Grouch went back into the house and planted his butt in a chair next to the bay window in the front of his house. He eventually fell asleep in the chair, with the outside lights on. Bud and John cruised by and parked a couple of houses away and waited. Then after enough time for the Grouch to be in a deep sleep, they quietly built a three foot wall of cement blocks across the street. Bud took three large firecrackers, tied them together, lit the fuse and stuck it through the Grouch's mailbox. When they blew-up the sound was like a hand-grenade going off in his living room! The guys made it back to Paul's porch without being caught.

The show from Paul's front porch continued when the cops came again and this time simply put detour signs up and left the Grouch to solve the problem of getting the cement blocks, now three feet high across the street, back onto his property. The local newspaper had an article with the headline "Pranksters Blow Mail Box," they saw the next morning. Then they watched the Grouch move the cement blocks, one by one, from the center of the street back on to his property. An entertainment they enjoyed with morning coffee on Paul's porch.

On another occasion, in the middle of the night, Bud was awakened by Paul knocking on the window of his room. When Bud opened the window, Paul said, "Your horses are out." Bud's mare, "Trouble," and her colt, "Double Trouble," were found on the San Gabriel Country Club golf course. It seems they were having great fun running and sliding across the putting greens. Paul helped Bud round up his horses and got them home before the damage was discovered the next morning. Paul was more friend than cop.

Bud graduated from High School holding the athletic honors for many years. His dad was extremely proud of his son and in 1947 he entered Bud in the 1947 Junior Olympics of

Southern California. One problem was he did not tell Bud. Without training for one year, it was a shock when his dad gave him the news. He was entered in the High Jump, and as a last minute replacement, in the 440 yard relay where each of four men run for 110 yards. Bud was the anchor man, the last of the four men on his team.

Although time had passed, Bud won the High Jump event to everyone's amazement, including Bud. In the 440 relay, he was the last to receive the baton from his team mate, coming from behind the other three competitors, his heart-pounding effort calling for all he had from his cowboy-strong legs; he crossed the finish line, won the race and fell flat on his face. John Cardos, Sr. was one, proud Papa!

To interject an important memory in Bud's young life, a few of those early friendships developed in and out of school days and lasted until life came to an end. Elliot, Walt and David were close buddies with Bud from the teen years and their adventures, parties and girlfriends and later the families, were all intertwined. Cowboy Bud remains the "last man standing" in this life but the bond of those early friendships are ingrained until and after, "the cowboy's last ride."

John Sr. bought a cabin in Big Bear, California. It is a community on the shores of Big Bear Lake high in the San Bernardino Mountains surrounded by a variety of tall, beautiful pine trees. Big Bear was a young boy's dream come true, particularly when Bud met and fell in love with his first horse affectionately named, "Trouble." They were meant for each other. Training of a horse by a young man is a two-way relationship. As their affection for each other grew, the bumps and lumps became less.

Cardos Cabin at Big Bear Lake

Bud with Trouble

Many Western Movies were made by Hollywood in those mountains. Bud got to know several movie stars without knowing who they were. He recounts riding with Peter Lorrie, a big star as a Character Actor. They rode together many times before Bud learned of Peter's fame. One of Bud's favorite memories is his attempt to breed "Trouble," his mare, to the Star Stallion of Cowboy Star, Roy Rogers, "Trigger." Bareback on "Trouble" Bud rode through pine trees at night to where "Trigger" was stabled but before he could get the horses coupled, he was chased off by watchmen not wanting the horses to mix blood. It was a wild night's ride heading for home!

One year winter came early in October with a blizzard-like snowfall. It caught the stables where young Bud worked by surprise. The conditions were so bad that Bud and his cowboy wranglers had to take their sixty head of saddle horses down to their winter stables by the old road that winds down the backside of Big Bear to the valley seven thousand feet below. With horses slipping and sliding on the pavement, the cowboys slowly made their way down the mountain. Then the snow turned to rain which continued for three or four hours into the darkness of night. Life in the saddle is a way of living. That night with horses trying to return to the home stables with severe cold and wet weather conditions was one of the toughest nights ever known to Bud and his fellow wranglers.

The ranches in the area are few and far between down the mountain. Bud asked first one and then another rancher for permission to hold the herd on private property for overnight shelter. For one reason or another they turned him down. After nineteen plus hours in the saddle, changing saddle horses on the way, a wet and cold, Cowboy Bud went to the front door of another ranch. An African American couple answered the door. The couple welcomed them out of the cold night, prepared food for them and changed the sheets in the spare bedrooms. The men, after corralling the horses, got a much needed nights rest.

The memory of those kind people left an indelible impression on Cowboy Bud. The Good Samaritans refused money for their help. Bud asked if there was anything they needed and they mentioned they could always use some firewood. When the horse-drive was completed and the horses were safely at their winter pastures, Cowboy Bud returned to Big Bear. About a week later he took it upon himself to take a load of firewood in the back of his 1937 Chevy to the couple for their thoughtful acts of kindness, people who let their actions speak louder than words. No one was home. A couple of weeks later Bud took another load of firewood to the Good Samaritan's ranch. He tried even a third time to deliver firewood. Each time he would leave the firewood by the back door. He never saw the couple again.

In fact, all the time spent in those mountains with his horse was a way of life that fulfilled Bud's young life. It helped him develop his values and personal principles. The people he worked with were all of the outdoor types from cowboys, cowgirls and movie stars. It helped Bud understand that movie stars are people, most being kind and friendly who enjoyed being known as, "friend."

Bud loved those teenage years. Although the family still lived in San Gabriel, they spent as much time as possible in those mountains. The Cardos Cabin was opened when warmer weather returned in Spring. John Sr., and his employees and friends from his restaurant in L.A., took the cabin. Bud and his buddies pitched tents outside. His heart was in those mountains. He and his friends would drive up from San Gabriel to Big Bear to get local gals to go to their High School Prom. There were special girlfriends for young Bud but none more special than his horse. It is the cowboy way, hard for some people to understand but it is true. And no girl likes playing second fiddle to a horse!

Pat Armstrong, from High School got more attention than the other girls and her brother became one of Bud's best friends. Much to Bud's surprise many years later, the phone rang one day and it was Pat as a grandma. She explained she couldn't ride anymore and insisted Bud take her saddle given to her by her Dad at her High School graduation. Shocked and pleasantly surprised, he gratefully accepted it. They met for lunch and enjoyed their trip down memory lane. Bud treasures the saddle and the memory of their youth together. In the early days after Pat moved east, Bud met a Big Bear gal, Joy, who shared the horsey lifestyle around The Twin Bear Stables and remained special for quite some time in Bud's life.

Cowboy Bud learned to play the guitar and became part of the local entertainment at the Big Bear Hotel and Chad's which is still the most popular bar in town. A town whose population was about two hundred people. The Peter Pan Lodge was located on the outskirts of town for the most affluent visitors. Bud would work odd jobs during off-season and could be seen riding his horse with a pick and shovel over his shoulder on the road when he was too young to drive a car.

Danger did not keep Bud from learning the trade of being a Rodeo Clown. If you have been to a Rodeo you have seen the clowns distracting bucking bulls when the riders were thrown. Bud recalls one time when the bull came close to putting an unwanted hole in his backside. "I kept running in a tight circle. The bull was wiping snot on my butt! He finally got distracted for a moment and I got control again. The audience loved it! They thought it was intentional and cheered!" Bud laughed. "Naturally, when I could, I took a big bow."

The clown's main job was to, one way or the other, get the crazed, bucking bull into what is called "the catch pen" and keep him from stomping on the thrown cowboy. One time the bull just trotted into the catch-pen nice and easy. Bud took a bow and unseen by him, the bull suddenly turned and charged. The audience was yelling. Bud thought they were pleased with the performance and took a bow at the exact moment the bull was just a few feet from him. He saw the bull out of the corner of his eye, jumped up grabbing the fence on the edge of the arena doing "a kip" just as the bull passed below him. The audience loved it! They thought it was all part of the act.

TV Series like, "Sargent Preston of the Yukon" starring Robert Preston and movies with both Roy Rogers and Gene Autry and with Bud mainly doing horse-work provided him with more movie experience. During the years in Big Bear riding his horse, clowning, singing at Chad's Bar and taking night rides with Joy, were the best years of Bud's life until one day a letter arrived to the young American; GREETINGS FROM UNCLE SAM! Cowboy Bud became a member of the United States Army.

Chapter Two
U. S. Army

There was mandatory service required to your country in the 1950's United States by any and all young men to join the Army, Navy, Marines or the Coast Guard after the age of eighteen. If you waited to be called as did Cowboy Bud Cardos, you got notified by the Draft Board. In Bud's case it was the U. S. Army.

Bud was busy with his life in Big Bear with his horses and clowning at Rodeos. He also worked in construction, building and remodeling homes in the area. Just before he received his letter to report to the Induction Center, he had an accident on the job. A skill saw slipped and cut a gash in his left leg causing one hundred and twenty stitches. A little further and he would have effectively sawed his leg off.

With the wound new in the healing process and both shoulders torn from Rodeo events, Bud reported to the Induction Center with the hope the Army would reject him as disabled. He wasn't faking it as he limped into the facility and showed x-rays from his damaged shoulders. He quickly learned the level of acceptance was, "If your trigger-finger works, welcome to the Army!"

Bud limped and gimped through Boot Camp, Fort Cook, San Luis Obispo, California. On a couple of weekend passes he managed to visit with his girlfriend, Joy, who had moved to the Northern California area; a pleasant change from marching drills and learning military courtesy. After Boot Camp on the USS Breckinridge, he was sent to Tokyo, Japan, with the 40th infantry Division and then to Korea.

The 40th Infantry Division was a National Guard Unit activated during the Korean War. Many of the officers were young men in their late teens and seen as just that by Bud. He had some trouble with military courtesy which gave him unwanted attention in the form of revoked privileges.

Welcome to the Army

On arrival in Tokyo as the ship pulled alongside the dock, young Japanese children waved and indicated they wanted the men to throw coins. Bud obliged. The guy standing next to him said something like, "Don't do that." Bud said, "I don't see why not" and threw more coins to the kids. The problem was the guy next to him was a lieutenant. The young officer grounded Bud for two weeks. When his unit arrived at their Induction Camp on the outskirts of Tokyo, everybody got leave to go to town, except Bud.

When the 40th Division got to Korea, Bud did go to town with a buddy, Harris, a good hearted guy who was handicapped with something of a twitch and generally somewhat uncoordinated. The men went to town seeking some female companionship. Bud recalls his "entertainment" cost him four cigarettes and a fountain pen.

Time got away from them. The curfew with zero tolerance was twelve midnight. Running through the rice paddies on the narrow paths, Harris misjudged and went head first into a rice paddy fertilized with human waste. Slipping, sliding and stinking, Harris and Bud arrived back at Base at four minutes after midnight. You guessed it. Bud was grounded for another two weeks.

There was something of a success story during Bud's service. While riding back to Base on a bus, he spotted a pretty, young girl smiling at him. He moved over to her and in spite of a severe language barrier, got her to accept going to the Base with him. Using a raincoat for disguise he smuggled the girl on to the base where she remained for a couple of weeks in a room behind the Supply Sargent's facility "entertaining" the troops.

Bud & Harris, Bud on guitar

Bud's assignment was to the Postal Service where he delivered mail to the men on the front lines. Delivering mail and Army life in general is not fun for anybody but barely tolerable for a man like Cowboy Bud who loved life, not killing and war.

The Korean War was toward the end when Bud was sent back to the States and mustered out of the Army at Fort Ord, California. For his temperament it would have been better to live in the days of the pony express but he did his job well and made the rank of Corporal. The day came in 1952 when he completed his Active duty.

He was transferred to Reserve Unit to finish the balance of his military obligation to Uncle Sam, a total of six years. In the history of America's wars the time was between the ending of the Korean War and Viet Nam. Bud did not have to return to active duty. The mandatory service to his country ended.

The best highlight of time spent in the Army was the healing that took place of his left leg and operations on his shoulders. Bud headed for home without a limp, and medically repaired shoulders from the Bronco-busting and Bull-riding days, compliments of the U. S. Army.

Chapter Three
Stars Are Born

Bud went directly home to his family in San Gabriel out of the Army and to work for his Dad at his restaurant. Civilian life was good, even better when a customer, a young lady, caught Bud's eye. It didn't take him long to learn her name, Barbara, and develop a close relationship that quickly turned to romance. It was not long before wedding plans were made.

Mom and Dad Cardos not only approved but helped Bud buy a three and a half acre ranch in Baldwin Park, CA. A date was set for the nuptials when tragedy hit. John Sr. died. The wedding and funeral were close together. The marriage took place knowing that was what John Sr. would want.

Life changed for Bud and Barbara. Mom Cardos took over the day to day operation of the downtown L. A. Restaurant and it wasn't long before Bud's Cowboy life began to give him the itch for the mountains he loved. Becoming a father not once, but twice in the next few years, delayed reaching for his dream. Two daughters, first Cindy and then Judy, were born to Bud and Barbara.

Work at the family restaurant continued until Mom Cardos decided to sell it and a little later, the family home in San Gabriel. Bud was able to talk Barbara into selling the ranch in Baldwin Park and move to the Cardos Cabin in Big Bear. At last Bud was where he felt was his 'belongin' place. He began his cowboy life again in Big Bear. Unfortunately for Barbara, it was not a lifestyle she enjoyed.

Bud kept life and limb together by working with horses in movies for Roy Rogers and Gene Autry and any movies filming in the San Bernardino Mountains, riding in rodeos and clowning for the crowds. At nights he would sing and play his guitar in Chads Bar and other local night spots in Big Bear.

Realizing his clowning act could be improved and on invitation from an uncle who owned a pet store in San Francisco, Bud flew to meet a potential improvement to his Rodeo Clowning, a Gibbon Ape. It was love at first sight. His name was Freddy.

Bud and Freddy Cardos

The immediate problem was how to get Freddy back to Southern California. Bud checked the various means of transportation. Both bus and train ended out of the question only allowing Freddy to ride in a luggage compartment. Bud decided to fly himself and Freddy to Los Angeles. To do this, Bud bought swaddling clothes and a blanket, had Freddy given a shot of tranquilizer and at the airport, passed him off as his son, Freddy Cardos. When the stewardesses wanted to see cute little Freddy, Bud would explain, "He's sleeping right now," keeping Freddy's face covered with the baby blanket.

In those days the airplanes used on the flight from San Francisco were DC-3s, a twin engine prop-job. The flight took about four hours. All went well until about three quarters of the way to L. A., Freddy started to squirm. Bud did all he could to contain Freddy in his blanket and swaddling clothes. The tranquilizer was wearing off. Suddenly a hairy arm shot out and across the mouth of a stewardess seated in front of them on the airplane. She had not been feeling well and was taking some oxygen when Freddy's hand closed on her mouth. As fate would have it, she just happened to have a pet monkey and didn't have the reaction one would expect, earth shattering screams! As a matter of fact, with her help and the captain of the aircraft, a first flight certificate was issued to Bud for First Flight for Freddy Cardos, signed by the captain and all the stewardesses. After landing, the local press met the airplane at the Burbank Airport. Freddy and Bud made the newspapers for a memorable moment and Bud left the airport with Freddy as quickly as possible heading for Big Bear.

———

Back when Bud first got out of the Army, his friend, Don Armstrong offered him a ride in a single engine plane. Don was a new pilot and landing at Van Nuys, CA, he managed to flip the airplane on its back. Don jumped out of the cockpit and took off running. Bud remained and without panicking, turned off the power and gas preventing fire. His idea of flying a plane was born.

Now some years later while Freddy and Bud were clowning at Rodeos and doing horse-work in movies, Bud decided to buy and fly a plane. He saw an ad for a Stetson Station Wagon and had the plane delivered to the little airstrip in Big Bear.

Never having flown a plane, Bud would run the plane back and forth on the air strip in Big Bear getting a feel of the "bird." With some lessons from a former, local fighter pilot instructor, the day came when Bud pulled back on "the stick" and got airborne. Flying high became a big part of his life.

Bud bought a book "Learning to Fly," and followed each step. The final part of training for his license called for a cross country flight. One afternoon wearing buckskin and cowboy boots covered with horse shit, Bud decided to do his cross-country phase of qualifying for his pilots' license taking off from Big Bear flying north towards Las Vegas.

In those days Las Vegas was not as metropolitan as it is today. From the air finding McCarran Field was much more of a challenge so when an air field was seen by Bud on his "reckoning" from ten thousand feet above Mother Earth, he decided to land. He made a good landing but noticed a vehicle that pulled in front of him with a sign, "Follow Me."

He had landed at Nellis Air Force Base. When Cowboy Bud climbed out of his plane to be introduced to the Commanding Colonel of the United States Air Force Base, he was fortunate to meet a man with a sense of humor. The Colonel just looked at this cowboy with horseshit on his boots, buckskin and cowboy hat and shook his head and said, "Young man, you are lucky we didn't blow you out of the sky." Bud simply thanked him as they went to the canteen for ice tea.

The Colonel gave Bud instructions how to get to McCarran Field in Las Vegas. He held up all flight deck operations while Cowboy Bud took off in his single engine plane dwarfed by the jet fighters and bombers on the Air Force Base. It was a memorable cross-country flight allowing Bud to complete his qualifications for his pilot's license.

Later in life Bud was making a flight from Los Angeles to Las Vegas at night. He speaks of some memories indelibly left on his mind about what has become a city known all over the world. In the early 1950s it wasn't more than a town of five hotels and a few small businesses. In remembering back through the years he told me when he was flying from L.A. at night he would come over the range of mountains separating 'the valley of the sun' as it is known and other inland cities. He said, "It looked like God had taken a handful of jewels and thrown them across the desert floor. It was strikingly beautiful. And you could buy a drink for fifty-cents and for about five dollars see the top headliners in all of stardom like Frank Sinatra, Sammy Davis, Jr., Dean Martin, Western Singing Star Patsy Cline, Louie Prima and Kealy Smith. You could walk down the street going from hotel to hotel and casino to casino with your drink in hand and nobody bothered you. It was a wide open party town." A warning: don't try it today!

Then a sad time came for the Cardos family. Barbara told Bud she was finished with his lifestyle. She wanted a divorce and custody of Cindy and Judy. In spite of love lost, Bud agreed to allow Barbara to have primary custody of the two young girls.

He had his pilot's license but the Stetson Station Wagon was in need of expensive repairs and with the break-up of his family, Bud didn't have the money. He horse-traded his way from pilot to a whole, new way of life and put his love of flying on hold. He went down the road with Freddy Cardos in a 1938 Chevy powered by propane or gas whatever was selected.

Bud and Freddy arrived in Las Vegas. Bud had ten cents in his pocket and the name of a Card Dealer, Ritz Campbell, at the El Rancho Vegas, a friend of a friend. Ritz turned out to be a life saver to Bud. He allowed Bud and Freddy to live with him and even gave Bud leads on possible employment.

The first place was a restaurant on the corner of Fifth Street and "The Strip" in downtown Las Vegas. Bud had his cooking utensils as a fry cook from working at his Dad's Restaurant in Los Angeles. The owner decided to give him a tryout and Bud passed with flying colors.

New friend, Ritz, allowed Bud to stay with him until he could acquire enough money to get a place of his own.

And let's not forget Freddy. Both man and trained Ape, Freddy Cardos, were shown the sights of Las Vegas by Ritz. In one gambling hall, Freddy decided to try what the people were doing. He got away and jumped from one slot machine to another pulling handles and having a wonderful time, not appreciated by some of the screaming lady gamblers or the security guards!

Chapter Four
Life Is Change

On a day off from cooking in the Las Vegas Restaurant, Bud took a ride in his Chevy to North Las Vegas to visit a saddle shop he had heard about. There was a man tending the store who was a friend of the owner but knew nothing about a saddle shop or its wares. The store-keeper had run off recently and as Cardos' luck would have it, a new man was needed. Bud took over the management of the store and after a few months of working two jobs, made arrangements with the owner to buy the saddle shop. Then, with thanks, he quit the fry-cooking job.

Under the name of Nevada Saddlery, Bud prospered. His product knowledge and true stories from his clowning, riding bucking horses and fighting crazed bulls made for good sales. Freddy Cardos was a good buddy but Bud found he was unable to give Freddy the attention he deserved.

A friend in Big Bear told Bud he would take Freddy and give him a good home. Bud took a couple days off to drive Freddy up to Big Bear. A six pack of beer was along for refreshment as they crossed the burning desert in Bud's old Chevy (long before air conditioning). Bud would almost finish a can of beer and give the rest to Freddy. Gulp and gone. By the time they approached the one stoplight intersection in Barstow the six pack of beer was finished.

When Bud stopped at the light, Freddy suddenly jumped out of the window onto the hood of the car next to them and began yelling and hopping from one car to the other paralyzing the traffic and effectively clogging the intersection. Finally with the help of the local cops, Bud got a hold of Freddy. With an apology and a bow from both, they went on their way with a wave, a proper ending to their relationship. Bud got about half of what he had paid for Freddy. He left him with his friend and in a good home in Big Bear and returned to Las Vegas.

One day at the Saddle shop a guy stopped by to browse the inventory. Bud got to talking with the guy and learned he had a Mountain Lion for sale and needed money. A short time later Bud was the owner of the pretty, young lioness. He began the nurturing process and named her Diane, meaning "The Huntress" in Greek mythology. She was a natural, highly intelligent lioness with a loving nature. She got big fast but even as a grown lion she was always just Bud's little pussy cat. They played together. The few scratches Bud received were accidental and never in anger.

The local police were friends and would stop by the saddle shop from time to time to visit with Bud and Diane. Bud lived behind the shop in a rustic, one bedroom apartment. One warm night, Diane decided to go on an adventure and dove through the screen on the apartment window. Bud called his police buddies. The word went out over police radios, "Bud's cat is out!"

One new patrolman and his partner about a half hour later were driving in a neighborhood alley when in his headlights suddenly appeared the shinning eyes of Diane. He slammed on the brakes and yelled over the radio, "There is a lion in this alley!" The cops forgot to make it clear that 'Bud's cat' was a lion! Bud quickly cleared up the misunderstanding keeping Diane from being shot. The local police learned to say 'lion" and not "cat" when referring to Diane.

About this time in Cowboy Bud's life, a long-time friend, Don Armstrong, showed up at Bud's saddle shop with his gal-friend colorfully known as, "Jungle Jenny," an animal trainer in her own right. Don knew Jenny and Bud would become good friends. And they did.

Jungle Jenny, Bud and Donald Armstrong — Sri Lanka

Jungle Jenny's story is fascinating and one of a kind in animal conservation, training and world-wide sales. Her dad traveled all over the world buying exotic animals: tigers, panthers, elephants and many of God's creatures ordered by circuses, zoos and the like. Jenny headed up the office in Los Angeles until her dad suddenly died. Customers and suppliers started calling from all over the world about their orders. Instead of closing the business, Jenny flew to Sri Lanka, loaded the order of five elephants on a gutted DC-3 airplane and flew them to the U.S. — an operation never tried before. The interior of the aircraft needed rewiring from fraying trunks but Jungle Jenny made the journey without the loss of life.

Another of many of her stories you can find in her fascinating little book, "Jungle Jenny," (Amazon.com) is while transporting a shipment of wild animals, a black panther managed to get out of his cage in the cargo area of a ship. With a stick and a whip, Jenny got the cat back in its cage. She carried the scars from the effort on her arm and hands for the rest of her life.

You can see why Cowboy Bud and Jenny bonded almost immediately. And Jenny was very much at home with Diane. Surprisingly, Don Armstrong was completely ignorant of animal training. He liked animals and even pressed Bud to let him take pictures of Diane. "Sure." Bud told him. All four jumped in Bud's station wagon and went off to Diane's playground in the desert.

What he did not tell Don was to "stand still." Don unintentionally started creeping around through the brush in Diane's playground to get the pictures he wanted. He moved cautiously with his camera poised.

What Bud did not explain was he and Diane frequently played a game of "tag." Bud would slink around in the brush and Diane would hide and suddenly attack Bud and jump up pushing him in the chest knocking him to the ground. With a wink to Jenny, Bud said "Watch this."

Sure enough, Diane came charging out of the brush and hit Don square in the chest knocking him to the ground. Don started screaming, "She didn't bite me! She didn't bite me!" Diane playfully romped off to another hiding place. Bud and Jenny were bent over with laughter.

Don Armstrong married Jungle Jenny and they remained friends with Bud through all of life. Later in their friendship, Bud even went through pre-production of the movie production of "Jungle Jenny." He got a money man to put up initial funding, hired a writer and flew to Sri Lanka with Jenny to see available locations for the movie. Unfortunately, the money man became severely ill and backed out of the deal. To this day, Cowboy Bud speaks highly of his friend, Don and his wife, Jenny. He has endless praise for Jungle Jenny, an amazing, young woman that accomplished so much with the animals of the world.

A very popular TV show in the day was, "You Asked For It." The production company came to Las Vegas to do a segment on Diane called, "The Lion Is A Lady." Briefly, the story line was Diane in an average American living room, sleeping on a rug in front of the fireplace. She dreams she is a Las Vegas showgirl. A Dissolve to: a long, white limousine arriving at the Dunes Hotel. The doorman opens the door of the Limo. Out steps a bejeweled Diane with diamonds for earrings, multiple necklaces and a bejeweled hat, her crown. She walked the red carpet that had been rolled out for her, majestically, and strolled into the Casino. Inside she is seen running a roulette wheel with her paw. A final close up on Diane. The camera pulls back and sees her surrounded by twenty-five show girls, the "Las Vegas Lady," the center of attraction.

An animal wrangler from the TV show, named Jim Danielson, struck up a conversation with Bud. The two men became fast friends. Jim asked Bud if he would be interested working with him on a TV show to be filmed in Independence, a small town in central California. Bud jumped at the chance offered by Jim, who became a good friend and a source for animal work in other movies. Bud left a young man in charge of his Nevada Saddlery, took Diane to a friend in his old, home community of San Gabriel and drove to Independence.

The job lasted a couple of weeks. Bud talked to the owner of the old hotel where they were staying and told Bud he could bring his lion and put her in one of the rooms on the second floor of the hotel. Bud went and got Diane and brought her to the hotel in Independence, California.

Bud put Diane in the second floor hotel room and told her to be a good girl. It was about midnight when he went to the bar where some of the men from the production crew were tipping a few. Bud joined in. A nice surprise was a woman vocalist singing. Her well trained, beautiful voice was equal to her natural beauty. Bud was hooked after the first song by pretty Helen Kay but he soon learned there was an obstacle, a boyfriend.

Bud had his guitar so when Helen would take a break, he would entertain with some of his country and western songs, a departure from the pop songs sung by Helen. Independence is a farm and ranch community. The audience loved him! By the end of the evening, Bud had caught Helen's eye and received a warm response.

Half drunk and tired from a long day, Bud bid all good-night and climbed the stairs to his room at the other end of the hall from Diane. He stripped down to his t-shirt and shorts, got in bed and was just about asleep when a terrible banging could be heard. Right away he knew it was coming from Diane's room. Upset and half-drunk he got out of bed, went down the hall, cautiously opened the door and there was Diane, slapping a chest of drawers from one wall to the other. Being on coasters, it would easily slide from one wall to the other. She was having great cat fun!

Her master, being in his weakened condition, angrily scolder her and put her on the bed telling her in no uncertain terms to go to sleep! Bud returned to his room, had just gotten into bed when the thundering sounds returned. Now really angry, he went back to Diane's room, slowly opened the door and — she was nowhere to be seen. He pushed the door open to discover she was in the transom above the door, her tail flicking back and forth. Bud grabbed it and standing in the hall still in only shorts and a t-shirt, commanded Diane, "Get down!", pulling her tail.

Across the hall a door opened and a very drunk man stepped into the hallway, took one glance at the sight before him and with a look of total misbelief, turned and staggered back into his room and slammed the door. No one ever saw the guy again. Maybe he stopped drinking not believing his own eyes! You can imagine him trying to tell people what he saw that night in Independence, CA. "There was this guy pulling on a lion's tail…she was in the transom above the door of the room…he was in his shorts and t-shirt…yelling." It would be certain he was not only drunk but crazy!

Bud worked every day as part of the crew on the TV series and by night continued to make points with Helen, in the hotel bar. His station wagon parked by the side door served as a love nest enough times over the week to ten days that followed. Helen chose Bud over the boyfriend who suddenly vanished from the scene. When Bud's work was finished with Jim Danielson, Helen went back to Las Vegas with Bud and Diane as a new member of the family.

Life with Helen was smooth, passionate and interesting for a while. She had family in Montana and Bud and Helen took a couple of weeks to make their way for a visit, by singing and playing guitar at one night stands there and back again. They had some good times but there was one of Helen's defects of character that Bud did not learn until later in their relationship. She was extremely jealous! Not the normal, protective nature of a woman toward her mate but crazy, insane, unjustified jealousy!

An example of Helen's unnerving and vicious, verbal attacks was one morning Bud went on an early dove hunt with his two close friends, Ritz and Paul. The best time to get the birds was at dawn so Bud said he should be home early. After the hunt, Bud spent time with his buddies and did not get home until about noon. Helen attacked him verbally calling him names that would make a sailor blush.

Another time she got on Bud's case about some imagined relationship and began screaming and yelling at him. He retreated to his station wagon. Moments later, Helen came out screaming obscenities, took a shovel and broke every window in Bud's 1956 Ford station wagon. He stayed locked inside covered with broken glass until she got tired and stormed off.

Needless to say it wasn't long before the singer with the angelic voice was given her walking papers, leaving Bud with the one loving female in his life, the beautiful, loyal lioness, Diane.

With Diane, it was never a quiet life but that was not always her fault. During El Dorado Week when the whole town was having a party, Bud, Ritz and Paul were making the rounds to the different clubs in downtown Las Vegas and they spotted Fess Reynolds, the famous Rodeo Clown, walking a toothless African lion down the sidewalk. Well, hell — if he can do it, so can we. They got Diane and came in the back entrance of the Mint Casino, an old Vegas landmark.

Once inside, Bud unclipped Diane's chain and let her go on an inspection tour; beginning by walking on the back of the booths, sending customers screaming out of the showroom. The guys made their way to an empty booth and sat down ready for more drinks not necessarily needing any more booze. Naturally, the hotel security arrived and escorted the four of them to the nearest exit.

Cats have a cunning nature. Cat owners will testify to their independence and intelligence. To illustrate this nature, an encounter happened in the back yard of Bud's saddle shop where he had Diane tethered on a twenty foot chain. A blow-hard guy came by with his German Shepherd dog and began to needle Bud to let him put his dog in Diane's enclosure to see what would happen. After multiple warnings, Bud allowed him to enter the enclosure with his dog on about a six foot leash.

Diane watched carefully as both man and dog slowly approached her. Putting her chain under her body and knowing exactly where the end of it was, Diane slid back, and back, and back. Quick as a wink she jumped forward and slapped the dog on the side of the head sending both man and dog flying backwards. Needless to say both of them left with their tail between their legs, both in body language and literally!

Diane with Liz Taylor's double

That illustrates the cunning part of the cat family. The independent part is well known by men all over the world whether they own a cat or not.

Chapter Five
Animal Wrangling

Nevada Saddlery was doing good business but to augment his income, Bud periodically worked construction jobs. After Helen Kay left him in a final rage, Bud gave a great sigh of relief. Between construction, managing his saddle shop and training Diane for public appearances in Las Vegas, he worked the honky-tonk saloons on Boulder Highway playing his guitar for ten dollars a night and all the beer he could drink learning not to miss a beat when beer bottles were thrown. He was a busy man.

Bud retained his close friendship with Ritz, the man who helped him survive when he first got to Las Vegas and another friend, Paul Wagner, who was a very famous glamour photographer in United States. The three guys decided to take a trip to the Grand Canyon. It became an adventure they were lucky to survive. They took the Nanquik Trail that was used for moving rustled horses years before. Time and erosion had deteriorated the narrow trail. A missed step and Ritz lost his backpack containing precious water and other supplies. Going three days without water, Bud dug a hole in the sandy soil in one of the side canyons. Thankfully, life-saving water seeped to the surface. They camped a full day by the water hole and survived on raisins and dried figs.

Paul and Ritz, Grand Canyon

To make a bad trip worse, when Bud got back from the adventure, his Nevada Saddlery Store was empty. The young man left in charge auctioned off or went down the road with all the contents. Another new beginning for Cowboy Bud.

Bud concentrated all his attention on the training and promoting of Diane. One evening while dinning at one of his favorite restaurants, he was impressed by the natural beauty of the young lady serving him. Her name was Pat. A few Cardos moves and a new romance blossomed. She wasn't a singing star or interested in the limelight of Las Vegas. She was happy just to be Bud's girl. It was a nice change for Bud. The change led to a marriage that would last for many years.

Animal Wrangler, Jim Danielson, from "You Asked for It," called Bud and asked if he would be interested in additional work as an animal handler. Bud jumped at the chance to work in movies again knowing one job might lead to another. He was right.

Through Jim different animal wrangling jobs quickly followed. First was "Overland Trail" starring Doug McClure where Bud doubled Doug. The action was a lion jumping from a cliff onto McClure, starring Diane; The mocking bird in, "To Kill A Mockingbird" Starring Gregory Peck; about 40 parakeets in; "If A Man Answers" starring Sandra Dee and Bobby Darin; the Buzzards in "Twilight Zone" with Andy Devine; The scorpion in, "Manchurian Candidate" starring Frank Sinatra; and some of the birds in Alfred Hitchcock's, "The Birds," to mention just a portion of the work.

Bud loved the creative process connected with making movies. He spent many hours observing how every department contributed to the effort besides the Actors and the Director. The Lighting Director, the Director of Photography, the First Assistant Director, in fact the total crew taking instructions from the Director for each new set-up and how the camera was used to move the story forward. Bud made a promise to himself he would someday, somehow work full time making movies.

Jim Danielson told Bud he could use some exotic animals not easily found in the United States and he would purchase a variety of them if available. He told Bud about the Palmetto Jungle outside of Mazatlan, Mexico. Bud and Pat left Las Vegas for the very unusual adventure with their baby daughter, Debbie. Pat drove their 1956 station wagon and Bud led the way in a paneled power wagon for hauling captured animals and birds.

About a week after their arrival in a small village near the Palmetto Jungle, Bud was able to hire an interpreter, "Chuy" who showed Bud around and introduced him to some of the local "Vacarros" (cowboys). They got invited to a rodeo on the outskirts of town. Young and old alike were taking turns riding young bulls. The crowd yelled encouragement at friends in their attempts to ride the bulls. "Chuy" was shouting at the top of his voice in Spanish. To Bud's surprise, he was shouting for the "Gringo" (Bud) to ride a bull. The crowd turned to see if Bud would accept the challenge. He did and rode the young bull around the arena until he stepped off and took a bow. From that moment on the "Gringo" Cardos could do no wrong. All the needed cooperation followed. The acceptance into their community helped Bud capture and acquire many boa constrictors up to eight feet in length (snakes), about fifty Iguanas one to six foot in length, two small Jaguar cubs and a couple of buzzards.

An incident on the streets of the small village caught Bud completely off-guard. He kissed his wife. Suddenly a local cop arrested him and took him to jail. There is a Mexican law not allowing a man to kiss a prostitute in public. The language barrier prevented any explanation. Pat (being dark-skinned woman) was able to find Chuy who was able to clarify and clear up the confusion. An unforgettable kiss to say the least!

Going across the border back into the U. S., the only crate that was questioned were the buzzards. The label on their cage was, "Black Birds." Fortunately, the Customs Inspector did not know a black bird from a buzzard. Buzzards are protected by a sanitation law in Mexico. They take care of road-kill and a balance in nature.

Jim Danielson bought all the animals and birds from Bud. Pat and Bud moved into a motel in the San Fernando Valley until Bud's work enabled them to find a furnished apartment. Hollywood living began for the Cardos family.

Chapter Six
The Hollywood Life

Bud worked different Movies and TV Shows as an Animal Wrangler with Jim Danielson experiencing the ups and downs of working in Hollywood. It is always "chickens or feathers." When jobs were not available in his chosen profession, Bud recalls, "Construction was booming in San Fernando Valley. The next day after finishing work on a movie, I could go to work on a construction job."

A big step-up in recognition for his various talents was the introduction to Al Adamson at the Hollywood Studios. Al had received the assignment to direct a Movie, "Blood of Dracula's Castle." It was a unique story of two vampires, a Count and Countess Dracula, several hundred years old that dinned only on the blood of young virgins, depicting the air of royalty in the process. Keeping a fresh supply was a challenge; a challenge met by several characters, Crazy Johnny (Bob Dix) The Butler (John Carradine) and Mango (Ray Young) the demented ghoul whose appetite was appeased by the used but not quite dead young girls in the basement of Dracula's Castle.

As Animal Wrangler, Bud supplied the rats in the basement prison and the bats which ended up being the eventual fate of the Count and Countess Dracula after being forced to face the morning sun. He also doubled the then elderly John Carradine in a fight between Mango and the Butler ending with the death of the Butler in a deep pit, the high fall done effectively by Bud.

That little, independently produced movie started a core group of workers, both in front of the camera and behind. One result was Dix International Pictures, a corporation formed by me. I invited Bud in as an equal partner and our attorney, Frank Saletri who received nine percent of the company for his services.

I wrote a fictional story entitled "The Greatest Treasure," about a psychiatrist on a pleasure cruise to Mexico. A private yacht with pretty, young girls in skimpy attire and handsome, hard-partying men of different ages heading south off the coast of Mexico. They drop anchor in a sheltered harbor away from any and all populated ports. The music blares as we see our doctor sharing a powerful fruit drink with a pretty girl. During a dissolve, the music ends and night becomes day with people passed out and scattered in different degrees of undress on the deck of the yacht in the morning light. The girl with our doctor moves from his embrace and staggers toward the wheel-house. Without waiting the necessary time for blowers to get fumes out of the engine compartment, she turns the ignition key. The starter grinds. In a long shot we see the yacht blow sky high in a ball of fire.

The only survivor is the doctor washed up on the shore of an isolated, Mexican Beach. Eventually he is discovered by a young Mexican kid, Poncho, who takes him to his remote village. His Mom and Dad welcome the stranger as does the whole family. The oldest daughter, Rosa, becomes the love-interest to "Cowboy," the name Poncho gave the doctor.

Some of our Hollywood friends came to Manzanillo, Mexico, to help us with the production. The Director, Bri Murphy, was on the rise as one of the best in the Motion Picture Industry as a woman Director of Photography having been the first to be accepted in the Photographic Union. She had come up through the ranks as a Script Supervisor, Production Manager, Editor and Cinematographer. She won international acclaim for her production of "The Magic Tide," as the Producer/Director. The story was centered on the twelve foot tide that comes up the Sea of Cortez in Baja, Mexico.

Our trip to Manzanillo was highlighted by some humorous events. One being when Bud's dog, Rusty, who weighed about 60 lbs, with all his papers in order for an American dog in Mexico, was being moved to the smaller, DC-3 aircraft for the last leg of our trip to Manzanillo from Guadalajara, Mexico. A rather small, Mexican, airport worker picked up the wooden crate that Rusty was in and began the transfer from Mexicana's jet from Los Angeles to the DC-3. A dance began as Rusty moved from one side of the crate to the other; a dance that went twenty feet in one direction and then the other. Bud and I applauded the Mexican worker. He never fell down but kept his feet under him. He finally made it to the cargo area of the DC-3 and put Rusty's crate on the ground.

That flight was equally memorable through mountain passes with running deer seen close on the mountain side and the Mexican passengers with their chickens and other farm animals on board. The landing on the dirt airstrip was rough but successful. The palm trees were all laid flat from a recent hurricane, quite a sight.

I played the part of "Cowboy." Our good friend and accomplished Actor, Steve Drexel and his sidekick, Sid, were the two "heavies" dealing drugs out of the remote, Mexican harbor. Both guys did a fine job. On the phone with Steve before his leaving Hollywood for Manzanillo, he asked me if there was anything he could bring. I explained the owner of our old, Mexican Hotel, a retired General, from the Mexican Army, who sat cross-legged by the Hotel entrance with two bandoleers of bullets across his chest and he loved comic books.

"Bring all the comic books you can find." "You're kidding!" Steve replied. I assured him I was serious. Steve brought comic books and from then on the General was our friend.

Bud played a pivotal character, "Alcatraz," named for time spent by the Mexican in the U. S. Prison. The dark skinned, Bud, made an excellent Mexican. As a matter of fact, Bud was sitting on a wall in the town near where we were filming in his character wardrobe as, 'Alcatraz." An American woman stopped and with broad gestures, broken Spanish and English tried to get directions to the hotel. Bud enjoyed the lady for a while and then explained in perfectly good English how to get to the hotel. The shock on the woman's face is remembered well!

Bud as "Alcatraz"

There are always stories during production of a movie, incidents that happened behind the scenes. One evening, after returning from a day of filming, we had an armed soldier ride on the fender of our vehicle going back to the hotel from location. We were under "house arrest" for not having a particular permit needed for filming in Mexico.

We had all the necessary, government permits but this was a local one. We all knew it was just another way to get money from "the Gringos" so Bri, our Director, went to town to clear up the problem. Stationed at several entrances to the hotel were Mexican Army soldiers with automatic weapons.

Bud and I being rascals always willing to surprise people, after a few drinks we jumped off the second story balcony on the side of the hotel to the soft sand below and causally walked by one of the sentries. We both said, "Buenos Noches," as we walked past. Being the stoic soldier, we didn't even get a nod.

We ran up to the second floor and jumped off the balcony again. We repeated the same action walking by the sentry saying, "Buenos Noches." This time the soldier not only blinked but gave us a "double take" not sure of his own mind. The third time casually saying, "Buenos Noches!", as we walked by. The soldier's mouth dropped open simply not believing his eyes. It was a fun gag and broke the tension of being under house arrest.

The point of the story was simple. The doctor known as "Cowboy" finally decides whether to return to his practice in Beverly Hills or stay with the heart-people that have come into his life. The usual answer is, "See the movie," but in our case our sound camera had gotten severely bumped in handling from Hollywood to our Mexican location and all our sound filmed scenes were in soft focus. The movie never made the silver screen. Considering our production plight, it is only fair to tell you that "Cowboy" chose his new family over the life he knew back in Beverly Hills, California.

Our second effort was entitled, "The Lonely Man," an original screenplay written by me based on the true story from the Old West. It was a portion of the life of a much feared gunfighter, Ben Thompson. The deserved fear by both the public and outlaws of the day like The Dalton brothers and Clay Younger and others mainly because Thompson had a death wish. He didn't care if he lived or died after being jilted by his true love back East. And he was a good shot.

My story included two characters both portrayed by Bud. "Little Joe," a half-breed and, "Satago," an Indian Chief leading a band of renegade Apaches and the half-brother of "Little Joe." Bud did an excellent job playing both parts.

Bud as "Satago" In Five Bloody Graves

The movie was directed by Al Adamson and co-produced by Al and Dix International Pictures. Al and I equally came up with the initial seed money getting us into pre-production and principle photography. We cast Paula Raymond as "The Madam," Scott Brady as "The Gambler," Jim Davis (of the TV series "Dallas" fame) and Ray Young as the "Gunrunners" and John Carradine as "The Preacher." I played Ben Thompson.

There is a scene in the movie where "Satago" and his band of Apaches attack a settler's cabin killing the settler and his wife and burning the cabin to the ground. On the screen, you see Bud as "Satago" charging toward the camera riding bareback with only a war-bridle on his horse. It is quite a scene with Bud covered in war paint playing the crazed chief.

What you won't see on the screen is when Bud's horse, a fast, powerful animal, decided to take a side trip and ran right up the ramp of the equipment truck. He came to a very sudden stop, spun around and jumped out of the truck. Bud being the excellent horseman he is, stayed on board. It was a scene I wished we had on film!

Besides shooting a Western in the beautiful country of Monument Valley, Utah, the memory of one early morning near Fruita, Utah, comes to mind. Bud and I were on horseback waiting for the delivery of promised funds arriving by private plane on the edge of a little dirt airstrip. We were anxiously concerned because we were out of money and owed our motel bill in the only motel in Fruita, Utah, the base of operations for our principle photography. The rest of the cast and crew did not know how strapped we were. When that plane popped up on the horizon, we both gave a nod and a sigh of relief. The attaché case with all the needed cash from Lamont Dupont Copeland, our major investor, saved us and allowed the completion of the production phase of the movie.

Part of the production responsibility was to provide first class transportation to and from location. I hauled a trailer with over ten thousand pounds of wardrobe behind my Cadillac from Hollywood to Utah. Bud, on the other hand, took care of transporting our stars on board his private plane. He would land in Cedar City, Utah, from the Van Nuys Airport, about a three hour flight. One of our stars had a fear of flying. The only way Bud got Jim Davis on board his 182 Cessna was about a half-gallon of 'screwdrivers' (vodka and orange juice). Jim never knew much about the flight and that was fine by him.

As an example of closeness between one of the dearest friends, Jim Davis and Bud became like brothers. It wasn't long after we all worked on, "The Lonely Man," Jim got the biggest break of his long career as an Actor in Hollywood. Some of you will remember his excellent performance as the father on the TV Series, "Dallas."

As fate would have it, while enjoying the pinnacle of success as an Actor, Jim was diagnosed with inoperable cancer. Bud was one of the first of Jim's close friends that was let in on the secret. To the very end, Bud would daily go to Jim's home and visit with him. Right up to the very last holding his hand as Jim passed on to the next world of God. The memory of the man, Jim Davis, is near and dear to our hearts always.

Our distributor, Independent International Pictures, found it necessary to change the title of our Western to, "Five Bloody Graves," because Paramount Pictures had a hold on the title, "The Lonely Man." They had a movie getting ready for production with that title starring, Jack Palance. Over time, our Western made its negative cost back on the world market and got into the profit column for Independent International Pictures, a company owned and operated by Al Adamson and Sam Sherman based in New York.

Bob as Ben Thompson, Bud as Little Joe, and cast of Five Bloody Graves

Chapter Seven
Satan's Sadists

"Satan's Sadists" was a movie produced in the late 1960s when it was popular to be anti-establishment. There was a feeling in our country that standards had changed. Corporate America and government, obeying laws and good citizenship, were old fashioned. Pockets of anti-social motorcycle gangs popped up across the country. Al Adamson and his partner in Independent International, Sam Sherman, exploited the sign of the times in the cult classic, "Satan's Sadists." There are several reasons why.

Independent International was able to get Russ Tamblyn of "The West Side Story" fame to play the lead bad guy, "Anchor." "Seven Brides for Seven Brothers" is another classic from his MGM days was another movie of great critical acclaim. Russ, playing a ruthless, indifferent, even crazy motorcycle gang leader was a total reversal from his past performances. Many were concerned that portraying such a ruthless character would harm his career.

One of the highlights of the movie was a brutal fight scene between Bud as "Firewater," and Russ as, "Anchor." In fact all of the gang members depicted individuals deprived of any good human qualities. It was the trend of the times. Accent was on selfish, animal traits. Bloody encounters, drugs and random sex were the order of the day for the motorcycle gang and the girls they picked up on the road. Even in the tag sequence when "Firewater" tries to tell the Marine Hero (Gary Kent) the danger is over, our hero attacks before hearing the news that all the gang is dead and their desert war is over. After a brutal fight, "Firewater" in a death scene is able to deliver his message of peace. Then through an expression of remorse seen on the face of our hero, he realizes what "Firewater" was trying to tell him. It was too little too late.

For contrast, in the first part of the movie we see a cop driving a convertible on a desert highway. On vacation, Scott Brady is traveling west with his wife and they give a ride to a hitchhiker, Gary Kent, a marine just mustered out of the Marine Corps. All the characters randomly happen to meet in a coffee shop and restaurant in the small community of Desert Summit.

That is when one remark leads to another and sparks fly when Anchor's girlfriend (played by Regina Carroll) starts dancing on the table tops to attract Anchor to her wares. She does anything and everything to get and keep Anchor's attention away from other girls.

The fine actor, Kent Taylor, plays the owner of the business who tries to appease the riotous gang and keep the peace, to no avail. When it is discovered that Scott is a cop, the hate Anchor and his gang have for authority takes over. Guns come out and all hell breaks loose. It ends with the gang taking Scott and his wife behind the business to a junk yard. Here Anchor, on top of a wrecked car, gives a speech about police brutality and then kills Scott the cop. During the chaos, our Marine escapes in a dune buggy taking the waitress from the restaurant with him. They take off across the desert.

Bud and I played two members of his gang. Bud, as mentioned before, as "Firewater" and "Willy" by me. We take up the chase along with five other gang members lead by Anchor. There are victims, orgies and death including a suicide by Regina Carroll when Anchor rejects her for another young girl.

Bob Dix as Willy (left) and Bud Cardos as Firewater (right) in Satan's Sadists

Our Marine (Gary Kent) manages, one by one, to eliminate the gang in a series of traps and maneuvers including throwing a rattle snake around Willy's neck and a knife thrown deftly into Anchor's chest. He and the girl from the restaurant are the only survivors.

With all the violence, sex and mayhem in the movie, once again an incident away from the cameras stands out. As in previous productions, Bud used his airplane to assist in finding locations and any needed service that would help with the principle photography. A stretch of highway outside the small, desert town was needed for a sequence in "Satan's Sadists." Permits were secured for Bud to land his plane on the highway from the California Highway Patrol.

When the time came to film the sequence, I parked my car across the highway at one end and another crew member parked his truck blocking the traffic at the other end. By radio I cleared Bud to land his Tri Pacer and he did. As he was taxing to the side of the road, a cop car with sirens blaring came screaming down the highway.

As happens, the Highway Patrol hadn't informed the local police of our permit to land. The first thing the cop said to Bud was that he was under arrest. "What about my plane?" asks a very concerned, Bud. "You'll have to take the wings off and trailer it out of here," is the response. Our hearts sank. Finally a call came through that we had been formally permitted to land the plane.

The pissed-off cop says, "Well get it out of here before I change my mind." Bud jumped into his plane, hit the starter and the battery was dead. Franticly we took the battery out of my car, fired up the Tri Pacer and Bud took off into the wild blue avoiding thousands of dollars having to trailer the plane to the nearest airport after taking the wings off. Making movies always have side adventures!

In spite of the raunchy story line, "Satan's Sadists," directed by Al Adamson and under the marketing genius of Sam Sherman of Independent International, grossed over ten million dollars in drive-in movie locations across the country and theaters elsewhere in the world.

It has become a cult classic by its audience acceptance and still is in demand from certain markets today. It brings to mind the different values asked for in entertainment through the years since WW 2 in our country. All successful movies can ever do is hold up a mirror to society. "Satan's Sadists" achieved that goal.

Gary Kent and Bud in Satan's Sadists

Chapter Eight
Japan

3D Travelogue

The author, Arch Obler, known for his many excellent articles written for the Readers Digest magazine, asked Bud to be the Unit Production Manager for a movie to be shot entirely in Japan in the then brand new 3D process. Using the honeymoon of a young American couple traveling the nation of Japan the new wide screen innovation would allow audiences to enjoy the beauty of the ancient culture as if they were there with the honeymooners. It was an extensive visit of forty-one cities.

Bud took the job of making all arrangements for the arrival of the Obler Production Company in each of the cities including housing, scouting locations needed locally and securing all necessary permits. Earlier in life, his Army experience helped with the culture. He knew he would need an interpreter to handle the language barrier and hired a young Japanese man, Keto, who became a good friend.

One of the first efforts was to get reliable transportation. Bud and Keto approached Toyota. With the Hollywood movie being produced in the nation of Japan underscored by the charm of "Cowboy Bud," the guys drove off in a four-door, Toyota convertible; a very special, VIP automobile reserved for royalty, high ranking military personnel and visiting heads of state.

There was a natural education for both men. Bud knew the importance of good manners from his Army days, particularly courtesy. There were sayings in Bud's vocabulary that just naturally popped out. Some would cause the young interpreter to stop in his tracks. One rainy day, when it was really pouring down, a cowboy saying came out, "It's raining like a cow pissing on a flat rock!" The young interrupter, Keto, bewildered says, "What you say?" "What you say?" "Cow piss on rock?" "Oh, flat rock?" "Piss on flat rock?" "Cow piss on rock!" On a dinner occasion, Cowboy Bud was cutting a steak, "This is tougher than an old boot!" "What you say?" "What you say?" "Tough as boot?" "Oh, touch as ol' boot!" And with a laugh Cowboy Bud speaking of a business value, "Money talks and bull shit walks." Poor Keto, "What you say?" "What you say?" "What you walk?" "Shit walk?" "Oh, money is shit?" "Oh, money shit?" "Oh, Got it, money bull shit walk."

Remembering, Keto, Cowboy Bud could not help musing about social situations that would confront Keto. He couldn't help thinking some rainy day would come when Keto would say to an elderly couple from the Midwest, being guided by him to some of the sights of Japan, "Cow pissing on a flat rock!" "Oh, It's raining like cow…pissing on flat rock." And he turns to the elderly couple with a big smile on his face.

From town to town and help from local publicity with photos of the Hollywood advance man coming to their area, Bud received a level of stardom of his own. Driving the four-door Toyota convertible rarely seen by the Japanese public, Bud became known. Pulling up to his hotel entrance, just being Bud, he would hop over the driver's door instead of opening it. Snap-brim hat with briefcase in hand, the image amused the doorman, "Oh, Mis'a James Bond!" The handle stuck and he became known by the hotel help and the press, as "Mr. James Bond." It turned out to be good public relations.

The 3D wide screen process went from a bang to a fizzle and today has been revived to a better level of acceptance. Still, it requires special projection and screen modifications along with audiences required to wear special, 3D glasses.

The Arch Obler incomplete movie of the young honeymooners traveling through the colorful cities of Japan is in a vault somewhere in Hollywood. Whether it even survived the post-production phase after principle photography was completed is unknown.

For Bud, the experience expanded his knowledge of people from another country and their lifestyle, beliefs and traditions. Lasting friendships were formed and to help the student exchange program, Bud took a young, Japanese student, Taka, into his home in Reseda, CA. The program supplied all needed support including transportation costs, a nominal wage and health insurance. For over a year Taka went to school, learned from our educational system and served as a "house-boy" to the Cardos residence.

After Bud had taken Taka on several flying trips to his cabin in the High Sierras and other destinations either for pleasure or movie work, Taka became enchanted with flying. Unbeknownst to Bud, Taka took flying lessons. He got his pilot's license and before returning to Japan he wanted to see the United States so he took advantage of a Greyhound Bus deal. For one hundred dollars he rode across the country getting on and off the buses for thirty days. He would get off the bus and then rent a plane, fly over the nearby countryside; an innovative, intelligent, young man. He sent Bud one of Bud's prized possessions, a picture of Taka as a Fighter Pilot by his Jet in the Japanese Air Force.

Taka and Japanese Fighter Jet

Cardos Export Company

While working and living in Japan, Bud seized a business opportunity he couldn't pass up. One day he was in the market with his friend, Ernie Singer, from the JPL Airline and asked the price in dollars of a cantaloupe. He was shocked to hear it was near twenty dollars. Bud told Ernie of the roadside farmers in California that sell a cantaloupe for ten cents. "Can you send me some?" asked Ernie. And Bud did. It was the beginning of the Cardos Export Company.

Back in the U. S. he made all the necessary arrangements to ship cargo containers with iced cantaloupes to Ernie in Tokyo. This led to other shipments. Bud would buy up fields of fruit in Mexico and later, vegetables. Ernie took care of the marketing end in Tokyo. If freshness became a problem with a particular shipment, it would be sent by aircraft. Cowboy Bud would on some occasions, fly his six-place, 206 Cessna south into Mexico. Landing on stretches of Mexican farm roads sometimes so narrow the airplane would have to be turned around by field hands, the fruit was put on ice, loaded in Bud's 206 Cessna and flown to the U. S. then on to Ernie in Japan by a commercial airline.

As an addition to Bud's life in between movie work, his export business added some good income. He and his actor friend, Roberto Contreras, well known star of the TV series, "High

Chaparral," would go to Mexico and Bud would buy whole fields of cantaloupes. They would meet the shipments that were trucked to the U. S. border with iced, large containers and then ship them overseas. Other fruits and vegetables were shipped until on one occasion the Japanese inspectors found a bug — one bug in a shipment. It led to a delay and like the domino affect; it affected letters of credit and the following shipments and the eventual demise of Cardos Exports. It was good while it lasted, about two years.

In travels back and forth from the U. S. several personal changes came into the life of Cowboy Bud, changes that would affect him for life. Part of world travel and movie work for Hollywood producers meant that home-life was spotty at best. Bud's wife, Pat and their children; Kimberly, Debbie, and their only son, John, Jr. met with a family tragedy. A fourth child was lost to an accident, a drowning when she was a toddler in the family pool; a little girl they named, Tammy. An accident is an accident but the loss of Tammy was the final blow to a marriage already in trouble. Bud was a good provider, father and husband but the time at home became more and more limited and husband and wife grew apart. The result was agreeing to disagree with Bud taking custody of their son John, providing a fully furnished rented house for Pat and the girls not far from the Cardos residence in Reseda, CA.

Bud and Ernie in downtown Tokyo

Night Walk

Well known and accomplished Director, Bob Clark, being aware of Bud's diversified talents for motion picture production, asked him to go to the small town of Brooksville, Florida. He asked Bud to be the production Manager, Special Effects Man, and Stunt Gaffer (coordinator) on a movie with the working title of "Night Walk."

Bud took the job and with his friend and assistant, Ron Coe, flew in Bud's plane, his six-place Cessna 206 to Florida. On the way with Ron, Bud recalls a fun time. He jokes about his Cessna 206 seeming to have a mind of its own when getting near New Orleans. Taking off about three in the morning, by five o'clock in the afternoon, the sights of the city were beckoning below. The 206 just seemed to circle the airport and land like a homing pigeon. In a short while, Bud and Ron were enjoying the sights and sounds of Bourbon Street. Bar hopping from one famous saloon to another, hearing the world class jazz played by the best, made for a wild time, a time remembered with aching hang-overs. The next morning they went on to Tampa, Florida, and Brooksville where Ron's wife soon arrived with Bud's son, Jon-Jon.

"Night Walk" starred John Marley, Lynn Carlin and Richard Beckas as "Andy" their zombie son. To give you an idea of the story, one review included, "An unsettling fusion of post-war drama and blood curdling chills." It was also released under the titles of "Death Dream" and "Dead of Night." The pictorial romp through fantasy helped Bud keep his focus on the here and now following the break-up of his family.

A local bar in the small town of Brooksville, Florida, was the social, collective center. As often happens when a Hollywood crew appears to make a movie, local tough guys tend to insult and challenge. Cowboy Bud was highly visible as the unit production manager and stunt gaffer. There was one guy who would not get off his case. The verbal insults followed by rude behavior, pushed Bud's patience until one evening while returning to his table with two drinks, the guy stepped in front of Cowboy Bud with another insult. Bud dropped the drinks and in one swift move, grabbed the guy by the shoulder and his crotch, and threw him up and over. The guy landed in a heap and incapacitated to say the least. After that, no further negative comments were made about the Hollywood crew and good ole' likeable Bud returned to his mostly pleasant personality, the way he had been known before that evening. He bought the guy a drink.

An added service to the production company developed when the trip to the lab in Tampa at the end of the work day added almost a three hour drive time one way from Brooksville. Bud would fly the daily exposed film to the lab and return with needed additional equipment after taking the six seats out of his plane or sometimes use his 206 to fly actors in from Tampa to Brooksville. "I use my plane like most people use a car. It was just faster," says Cowboy Bud. "And I got all six seats upholstered with the extra money."

During the stay in Florida, a pleasant surprise brightened Bud's life, Kazuko Kamibeppu, a girlfriend from Bud's many trips to Tokyo, arrived in Tampa. Bud flew his plane to Tampa, picked her up and returned to Brooksville remembering one thing he said to her, "You have flown from Tokyo to Brooksville, Florida, with only one stop. Half-way around the world! That's 'a first'!"

Kazuko set up housekeeping in Bud's hotel room in Brooksville. Being a great cook, she made the motion picture crew happy, both guys and gals. It became obvious she was an industrious girl. One morning Bud woke up to the sound of a lurching automobile in the parking lot outside his window. Kazuko was learning to drive in Bud's company car so when she returned to Japan, she could get her driver's license, a difficult task there. Bud took over the driver's education.

Bud's personal life was colorful to say the least. A beautiful actress from South Africa kindly left Bud's hotel room when 'Kimbeto' arrived and after she left for Tokyo, the lovely lady returned being a very accommodating, friendly friend. Her gift to Bud was unlike the Zombie theme of the movie he was working on. His life was that of a happy man!

Every Hollywood company does not always leave a community with a good impression. Cowboy Bud always reached out to the local population with the hand of friendship. He always ate and drank with them and never let people think he was any different from them. It always takes time to be accepted because people have the impression that Hollywood people tend to be snooty. When Bud finished his work in Brooksville, there were hugs and handshakes all around.

Mark, the Sound Man on "Night Walk," and friend since the Tokyo 3D Travelogue, joined Bud and the Script Supervisor for the flight in his 206 Cessna back to California. A trip that was marred by a horrendous rain storm forcing Bud to land at a remote air strip where they were grounded for hours with three inches of water on the runway.

Bud recalls reminiscing with Mark about a time they shared while making the movie in Tokyo. With some time to kill before a production meeting, Bud and Mark went sight-seeing and came across a Japanese bar just opening at four in the afternoon. The men went inside and enjoyed the very oriental décor along with a large jug of Saki, the powerful, Japanese drink served pleasantly warm. The guys drank it and another.

When it came time for the production meeting back at the hotel, Bud went to Mark's room and found him passed out in the bath tub. He pulled the plug so Mark wouldn't drown and went to the meeting. With all the water around them on a lonely airstrip somewhere in the middle of America, they laughed at the memory. "Remember when I saved you from drowning?" Bud reminded Mark. The two men remain close friends from that day to this.

When the weather cleared enough for a take-off, Cowboy Bud put the 206 into the wind and headed west for California.

Chapter Nine
Stunts and Bumps and Bruises

Bobby Rose, one of Hollywood's best known stunt men said, "They don't do stunts anymore. They do bumps." Cowboy Bud always did stunts as anyone who worked with him can testify.

Bud laughs when people ask him about his first stunt. He jumped into a Little Red Wagon with his cousin and they went through a ring of fire in the backyard of the Cardos home in San Gabriel mentioned in the first chapter of this book. What it led to in Bud's life begs the line, "Truth is harder to believe than fiction." The best we can do to honor his work without writing a separate volume about "Cardos Stunts," is to give you highlights of some varied stunts with horses, fire, fights, cars, people and planes.

In our Western movie "Five Bloody Graves," Bud did several stunts. He bulldogged the double for Jim Davis off his horse at a dead run. Bud has a saying, "If I can get a hand on a horse, I can get on him." You might mistakenly think he means a hand on the saddle. No. If he can get a hand on any part of the horse as it runs from him, he will get on the horse — well, within reason.

Bud and I staged a fight at the end of "Five Bloody Graves," that took us from a knife fight down a hill and into a river.

Five Bloody Graves, Bob and Bud in knife fight

The fight continued in the water until Bud as the Indian Chief "Satago," goes over a waterfall to his death. As Ben Thompson, I managed to drag an exhausted body to the rocky, river's edge and collapse. An unseen factor, and with stunts there are always unseen factors, the river water was melted snow high in the mountains of Utah.

In the horror movie "Blood of Dracula's Castle," Bud did a fire stunt. He wrapped his upper body in aluminum foil, put fire accelerant (a mixture of lighter fluid and a small portion of gasoline) on the clothes that represented "Mango," the demented caretaker of the castle, poured the accelerant on his upper body and the assistants lit him on fire. The two men that held Bud's life in their hands were long-time friends and crew members, Forest Carpenter and Ron Coe. The camera rolling, Bud staggered to the edge of a cliff and appeared to go over the edge. When Bud falls to the ground, it is the cue for the men to run into the scene and put out the fire with extinguishers and blankets. A smoldering Bud immerged with a wave to the crew that all was OK.

It has already been mentioned that Bud doubled John Carradine who played "The Butler," in the same movie and took a high fall to a cellar floor about twelve feet below. Every stunt done takes knowledge, coordination and careful preparation. It is necessary to have proper padding on the body and some form of cushion, when possible, for the fall. Timing and physical condition are essential. Rehearsal for the camera is limited without doing the actual stunt. The stuntman has worked out the details in his preparation to eliminate possible injury. The result can be death or permanent disability if mistakes are made.

Jumping out of a moving car before it goes over a cliff to destruction is nerve racking to say the least. Bud's crew (usually Forest and Ron) would carefully tape sponge rubber to any and all door knobs and all potential exposed window cranks that could snag clothing. On independent productions where money is tight, actors are asked to do dangerous scenes. Bud has been Actor, Stuntman and Director in many of his movies, one job or all, whatever was needed.

Another job description is "Stunt Gaffer," a term given to the man in charge of all the stunts in a movie. He is responsible for all the planning of every stunt connected to the production so that at no time the production is held up while stuntmen figure out how to achieve a particular dangerous action needed for the story. Cowboy Bud has been the "Stunt Gaffer" on movies produced in the United States, Canada, Africa, and elsewhere in the world.

Here are some the highlights from Bud's memory over many years of movies and TV shows he worked on. In many cases, as mentioned, he contributed in several other production jobs like acting, assistant director, unit production manager, associate producer, stunt gaffer, stuntman and later in his career, Director.

As "Firewater," in "Satan's Sadists" there were two grueling fights in the rocky hills of the lower, California desert country. One between "Firewater" and Russ Tamblyn, as the lead bad guy "Anchor;" and one between Gary Kent as the "Marine," the leading man in the story. The two fights together took at least ten minutes of screen time and created fans for Bud writing to him from many places in the world about his role as "Firewater."

As the "Federal Agent" in "The Road Hustlers," where he and his partner, Bill McKinny, (in his first movie role, propelling him to a very successful career as an Actor working with John Wayne, Clint Eastwood and others) the two "Federal Agents" were constantly tricked into one situation after another by the Moonshiners, consisting mainly of the Reedy Family with Jim Davis as the father of three wild-driving sons. Behind the scenes, Bud created seven car crashes performing the dangerous stunts himself. And doubling me in a water-skiing sequence (as Mark, one of the sons) Dynamite was tossed by Scott Brady and another bad guy in the story, exploding around Bud. On one mistimed toss, it went under Bud that raised him up out of the water. He managed to land on his skis and kept going.

Road Hustlers, Jim Davis and Bob Dix

Cowboy Bud played an Indian in "Savage Seven," starring Robert Walker, Jr. While riding a horse in battle with a motorcycle gang, he takes a fall off the horse followed by a motorcycle crash by one of the bad guys next to him. They had to keep their heads down as motorcycles were flying inches over their heads. One of those unexpected aspects of the collective stunt was the motorcycle still in gear and idling, with knobby tires slowly grinded the first layer of skin off Bud's belly. It was a time when he was damned if you do and damned if you don't. Bud kept his head down and accepted the grinding. Bud spent the next couple of weeks with salve and gauze wrapped around his midsection wearing his pants just tight enough to keep them from falling off.

As a "Federal Agent" in Dick Clark's "Killers Three," Bud did a stunt crashing through a glass window. It was early in a friendship between Bud and Dick Clark that would last on and off the movie set for many years.

With Cameron Mitchell in "Nightmare in Wax," Bud doubled Cameron in a scene where as he lit a cigarette with Actor Barry Kroger (playing the bad guy), throwing brandy in his face, Bud burst into flames, spun around and crashed through a sliding glass door ending up in the swimming pool, a wet end to the flames before burning Bud's flesh.

Bud and Cameron Mitchell, Nightmare in Wax

Mentioning some of staged, movie fights among many, in the years of stunt work by Cowboy Bud would have to include the one in, "Hell's Angels on Wheels." He and fellow Actor and Stuntman, Gary Kent, were featured in a fight in a bar between two rival gangs totaling twelve men crashing over tables, angled punches in the head and face (angled for camera allowing for the punches to miss). This work starts as a dance in slow motion, each fighter knowing what to expect next and then sped up when going for the "take" before camera.

Mistakes are made and broken noses, cracked ribs, loosened teeth and bruised jaws do happen. Bud personally avoided serious injury but had his share of bumps, burns and bruises. Some of Hollywood's stuntmen have not been as fortunate, some killed and some crippled for life.

In "Flower Children," starring Adam Rourke and others, Bud staged a fight where he doubled Rourke in a fight with three guys. The three against one had to be choreographed carefully to avoid missed cues. The tag of the sequence was Bud being knocked back into an empty swimming pool. Even with knee, elbow and hip pads, a six to eight foot fall can be very dangerous to the stuntman falling on concrete. Fortunately for Bud, a few bruises but nothing too serious. A hot bath after work, promoted needed relief.

In another sequence in "Flower Children," Bud and his buddy, Gary Kent, staged a fist fight in a wrecking yard that received a lot of mention from the Stunt Man's Association and movie buffs everywhere. Again, every punch or kick, given or received were carefully rehearsed. The memories from the fight put the hot wrecking yard at the top of the list. It's hard enough to give and receive kicks, punches and taking falls in the dirt, but doing it in the heat of reflected sun off the metal wrecks puts sweat in your eyes!

As sophisticated as audiences are today, the speed of the action associated with a stunt takes place in real time along with the angle of the camera and the distance from the camera to the action, all important factors to any and all stunts. Like the time in Bud's many stunts with his lion, Diane, while doubling Doug McClure who starred in the TV series, "Overland Trail," also starring William Bendix, the audience saw a wild lion jump off a cliff on to Doug and take him to the ground. In fact, it was Cowboy Bud and his well-trained pet, Diane.

Another Cardos stunt called for Bud to take a fall from above the first level of an apartment building window into a four by six-foot trash bin. What made it different was Bud put the leading man, Paul Mantee, in a corner of the trash bin and promised not to fall on him. The star of the movie trusted Bud and as a result he was able to pop up after Bud made the fall without a cut or cheat in the action. On screen, only the cast and crew and a very happy Director knew the difference. It looked like Paul made the fall.

In, "Deadwood 76," Cowboy Bud played an Indian in addition to one of two cowboys that violently raped an Indian girl. He set up many the action sequences including performing horse-falls. It was an Arch Hall, low budget production, starring his son, Arch Hall, Jr. Production values were achieved without the usual camera car and other equipment for a major studio production. In one action sequence the Director wanted a close shot of horses at a dead run pulling a wagon.

Bud got the cameraman to sit in the trunk of the Director's Cadillac with his camera. With a warning to the driver to keep the speed of the car exactly at thirty miles per hour,

Bud climbed aboard the wagon with a final word, "Do not stop fast or even slow down or the horses would be in the back of the Cadillac!"

He drove the team at a dead run inches away from the trunk of the car creating a terrific action shot. Kudos to the cameraman, Lou Guinn, who didn't close his eyes with a galloping team of horses a few feet from his lens!

As an aside, I was hired by Arch Hall to play Wild Bill Hickok in the story. A real thrill for me, as my dad, Richard Dix, played Wild Bill in the Western, "Badlands of Dakota" (Early 1940s). I was able to get the same wardrobe from Western Costume Company in Hollywood Dad wore many years before.

By now you realize how diversified Bud was in all aspects of stunt work from horse-work, staging fights, car wrecks, high falls and more. His success was really based on his natural, athletic ability, the rest on acquired knowledge through the years of movie stunt work balanced by courage and self-discipline.

There are many co-workers in Hollywood that have their particular memory of working with Cowboy Bud. One production manager, Jack Boyer, has many such stories. Like the time Jack was saddled with a female Director shooting a Western in Old Tucson, an often used location for historical stories. Jack called Bud for help for a few days which ended up being more like three weeks. He ended up re-shooting and staged all new action sequences including a barroom fight. In the different horse sequences Bud directed different horse stunts. Those cowboys did not know about Cowboy Bud. They just knew him as the Action Director. At a gathering of the guys after principle photography was finished, they suggested Bud could direct stunts but could he ride a horse? He and Jack Boyer were sitting on horseback. Asking Jack to step off his horse, Bud rode a 'Roman Ride' (one foot on each of the two horses) around the arena leaving no doubt of his ability to not only direct but to perform. He reined up to applause and respect.

John 'Bud' Cardos Roman Riding

Numerous other movies like the work Bud did in, "Dunwitch Horror," starring Sandra Dee and Sam Jaffe. Bud was the Art director and driver of several car wrecks always assisted by dear friends, Forest Carpenter and Ron Coe who rigged the harnesses and necessary belts that protected Bud from serious injury. The dependence on these two men was absolute and Bud always tells people how he probably would not be around if it was not for those two guys and other dedicated crew members.

Remembering the Cardos stunts through the years, it would be remiss not to mention the Cowboy Actor, Producer, Director and friend of Bud, John Carpenter. John was one of the unsung heroes behind the scenes. He took it upon himself to become "the Cowboy to kids with special needs." He would make mini movies with the kids playing parts of the sheriff, the mayor, the good guys and the bad guys. His ranch was a playground for riding horses and enjoying the outdoors disabled children don't usually see.

Bud would help doing stunts, whirling horses around and taking horse-falls. After a full day of performing ten or twelve of the grueling stunts, an exhausted Bud made it home to enjoy a hot bath at the end of a long day for very little money to help John Carpenter and his kids. Cowboy Bud slipped getting out of the bath tub and broke his wrist.

He went to the ER and they put a splint taped firmly to his wrist. The timing could not have been worse. The next day Bud was to interview for the job of Stunt Gaffer on Arch Hall's, "Deadwood 76." He took the splint off his wrist and kept the appointment offering his usual deal, "If I don't save you my wages, you don't have to pay." He was hired. He left, went around to the back of the building, and threw up in the flower-bed from the pain in his wrist.

Fortunately, there was enough time spent in pre-production work, scouting locations and arranging for accommodations for the cast and crew and making the necessary deals for production of the movie that Bud's wrist was almost completely healed in time for principle photography.

As you know, flying was a large part of Bud's life. He used his plane in many unusual ways. One adventure worth mentioning was Bud's work on "Born to Buck," the outdoor, adventure saga rounding up horses for Casey Tibbs with Monty Montana, Slim Pickens, Joel McCrea and Cowboy Bud. The men were having trouble getting the large herd to turn into the valley from the canyons where they ran wild. It was the first time Bud used his plane to herd the horses. Flying very low, he used his aircraft to turn the herd, at one point dipping his wing within six feet of the ground. Casey said, "Now that's a first, a plane herding horses!"

For Al Adamson, Bud used his plane in a movie starring Charles During and John Gabriel in a drug smuggling sequence and in, "Kingdom Of The Spiders," directed by Bud. He used his plane to photograph spiders crawling all over the pilot played by stuntman, Whitey Hughes. It was a very scary and dramatic scene as the spiders eventually cause the pilot to go crazy and crash.

The time comes for everyone who is a pilot when common sense dictates an end to flying. Cowboy Bud made the decision at age eighty-four after flying his various airplanes since 1952. Having owned sixteen different airplanes and over 7000 hours in the air, he had made only three emergency landings. It closed his career as a pilot with a spotless safety record. Only Cowboy Bud knows how many near fatal flights making movies were involved. You can bet there was more than one!

Chapter Ten
Canada

From Cowboy Bud's work on, "Night Walk," in Florida, Producer, Bob Clark and Director, John Trent (both Canadians) offered Bud work on a production in Canada.

Sunday In The Country (1974)

To meet the requirements for a work permit in Canada, Bud was hired as "Special Effects" and "Stuntman" for the production of "Sunday In The Country," starring Ernest Borgnine and Michael J. Pollard. Briefly, the story is about three vicious thugs who are on the run in rural America after robbing a local bank. They seek refuge at the home of a reclusive farmer, but he is prepared for their arrival and holds them at gunpoint. While waiting for the law, he decides to take them into his cellar and torture them before the police arrive.

One way Bud handled his responsibility as a father leaving for a distant location was to go to Jon-Jon's school and get the school work needed for the next few months and take it with them, in this case, to Canada. Jon-Jon was able to be with his Dad on distant locations and keep up with his school work.

Likeable and friendly Ernie Borgnine and Jon-Jon began a lasting friendship on, "Country." For example, Bud's rule regarding donuts on the set in the mornings was one and no more for Jon-Jon. Ernie and Jon-Jon would each take a sugary, jelly donut and walk out the stage door. When Jon-Jon finished his, Ernie would give him his donut. When Bud found out about the "donut conspiracy," he let it go. The secret was safe.

Ernie Borgnine and Jon-Jon

News of the marriage in Los Angeles of Bud's daughter, Judy, reached him in Canada. Bud and son Jon-Jon were flown by Air Canada for the wedding. Bad weather provided terrible timing causing a delay of the take-off and grounded the plane. As soon as possible, the pilot got the plane airborne and, speaking from the cockpit, talked to the people performing the marriage explaining they were coming in as fast as possible and to please hold the marriage ceremony for Dad's arrival. Bud and Jon-Jon changed into their more formal clothes on board the aircraft to help save time upon arrival. Movie star Ernie Borgnine having become a good friend of Jon-Jon, helped him with the change.

They missed Judy's marriage by ten minutes. Bud was furious with the people at the marriage mill. Suffice it to say, words to the ministers and company from Bud sizzled the ears of the management. A loving hug and kiss from daughter Judy was all that cooled Dad Bud. The moment of missing his daughter exchanging her marriage vows is still a big disappointment, a three thousand mile flight to miss the wedding by ten minutes.

It Seemed Like A Good Idea At The Time

By now the Canadians were fully aware of Bud's many talents far exceeding just "Special

Effects" and "Stuntman." Starring in, "It Seemed Like A Good Idea At The Time," was Stephanie Powers, Yvonne De Carlo, Anthony Newly, Isaac Hays, Lloyd Bochner and the introduction in his first of many roles, John Candy, the wonderful comedian. As a Canadian comedy, the movie "Idea" received mild reviews for the story line but the Actors all received good comments.

Among memorable moments from behind the scenes, are a few that are worthy of remembering: Yvonne De Carlo and Bud collectively cooking a turkey and all the trimmings to celebrate the American Thanksgiving there in Canada. One night Stephanie Powers came to Bud and said, "Come with me." She led Bud to her dressing room. There stepping out of the dim light was, Bill Holden, the world-famous movie star and long-time lover to Stephanie. That was a wonderful moment for Cowboy Bud who highly respected Mr. Holden's work and good, lasting friendships were born that night in Toronto, Canada.

On the work front, a highlight from "Idea," was the rigging of a life-sized sculptor of Lloyd Bochner that world renowned sculptor, Paul Sevehone, created hollowed out to fit the Actor so according to a story point, a shotgun blast fired by Yvonne De Carlo blows the wax cast off Lloyd Bochner. Bud lined the wax sculpture with squibs (small explosives) and baby powder in thirty small bags. The explosion was perfect, leaving the unharmed Actor beneath a white cloud of powder — in long underwear.

Lloyd Bochner in Seemed Like a Good Idea at the Time — 21 squibs blow at one time

Paul Sevehone and Bud became friends working on the special effects for "Idea." When it came time to head for home in California, Paul asked for a ride with Bud in his plane with a request to stop in Las Vegas. He wanted to show him some of his work in the Art Gallery at the MGM Grand Hotel. Bud asked Paul to join him as his house-guest in California before visiting the MGM Grand in Las Vegas. Paul was delighted to accept the invitation from his new friend.

Upon arrival at the Cardos home, Paul was greeted by Barbara, the current lady-friend of Bud caring for his home, and an unusual animal for residential living, a pig, weighing close to 400 pounds penned on one side of the Cardos home. Barbara had developed a supreme fear of the pig and had only been feeding him out the bathroom window.

An ultimatum was given that was close to, "The pig or me." It motivated Bud to seek a friend with a pick-up truck. He called around with no success so with the usual Cowboy Bud finding a solution to the problem of getting the pig to the to the slaughter house, he, Paul and a couple of neighbors got the pig in the back seat of Bud's dune buggy.

They tied the pig down and to secure him further, Paul got on his back. It was an orange dune buggy with Bud driving and Paul on the pig's back driving along Sherman Way in Reseda, CA, heading for the slaughter house. Imagine yourself seeing such a sight. "Ride 'em cowboy" was one of the kinder remarks yelled at the trio.

Bud flew Paul to Las Vegas to keep his promise to see the art gallery with Paul's paintings in it. When they got to the MGM Grand Hotel and Bud saw some of Paul's work, he was very impressed and told him so. Paul took one of his paintings marked for sale at thirty-five hundred dollars off the wall and gave it to Bud. It was an interpretation of Greek Mythology that still hangs in the Cardos home today.

You can imagine the Frenchman having worked with people like John Candy, the crazy comedian, the movie stars like Stephanie Powers, Yvonne De Carlo and the other stars of "It seemed Like A Good Idea At The Time," and riding a four hundred pound pig on Sherman Way Boulevard in the back of Bud's dune buggy, certainly justified his last comment to his friend when leaving for France at the Los Angeles International Airport, "You are one crazy, California Cowboy!" Paul and Cowboy Bud are still friends to this day.

Although uncredited, Bud received excellent reviews for his work on, "Idea," as Second Unit Director, Assistant Director, Special Effects and Stuntman. Some movie makers forget what William Shakespeare said, "The story is the thing." Using a term in the insiders group in Hollywood, an "Idea" was not "released"— it "escaped." The poor reviews did not hurt Cowboy Bud or his reputation as a very valuable man on a movie set. In fact, he was invited back to make his next movie in Canada.

Find the Lady

Director John Trent by now had become totally convinced of Cowboy Bud's talents after working on several movies together. Although to continue to work in Canadian produced motion pictures meant Bud formally still was hired as the Special Effects and Stuntman and, as before, performed many other tasks on his next Canadian Movies.

"Find The Lady" was John Candy's second film on his rapid approach to fame. Mickey Rooney headed up the substantial cast of both Canadian and American Actors. The storyline was about the daughter of a wealthy businessman who was kidnapped. The Chief of Police, under a lot of pressure to find her as soon as possible, assigns officers Kopeck (John Candy) and Broom (Lawrence Dane) to track her down. None of the police know the girl's father had staged the kidnapping to pay off some of his gambling debts. He hired a couple of mafia goons. Unfortunately for him, the goons get the wrong girl. To complicate matters, the girl ('Lady') decides to run off with her boyfriend. To complicate matters even more, the girl really does get kidnapped and a third party is holding her for ransom. Somehow, the two bumbling police officers have to find their way through the mess and, "Find The Lady."

On the sound stages in Toronto, Canada, Bud recalls a most unusual event ever witnessed on the set of a motion picture. In between the actually filming of the scenes before the camera, the great entertainer, Actor and Dance man, Mickey Rooney, would read from a book entertaining the cast and crew by playing all the parts in the story with vocal changes for each character. He would literally do this daily, hour after hour. To this day Bud highly respects the fine talent of Mickey Rooney.

The next two Canadian Movies were produced most unusually. Bud worked on two movies at once moving from one to the other on prearranged shooting schedules by Director John Trent.

Breaking Point

Vincent Karbone, played by John Colicos, is a leading construction magnate in Philadelphia and a suspected leader of one of the city's most notorious, criminal gangs. Several of his thugs are on trial with the key witness against them being a judo instructor and mild mannered family man with a wife and kids, Michael McBain, played by Bo Sevenson. Karbone stops at nothing to keep his men out of prison and Michael's family becomes the object of his quest. The cast is joined by well known, American Actor, Robert Culp as Frank Sirrianni.

It was Robert Culp who became a fan and friend of Cowboy Bud while witnessing a stunt that included a house falling over a cliff. Bud had it rigged so by releasing cables and allowing the house to creak, crumble and slowly slide over the cliff, a most dramatic scene unfolded and with the adding of effects and music, one of the most memorable stunts still remembered to this day; all in all, a good action movie.

The Last Resort

A break in Canadian production took Bud to Catalina Island off the coast of California to do the stunts and special effects for an American International Picture entitled, "The Last Resort," with Ron Coe doing the special effects. Briefly, the storyline is George Lollar takes his family on vacation to "Club Sand," a shoddy and untrustworthy company. On their tropical island, they find soldiers everywhere, an unhelpful staff, inhospitable accommodations and undesirable holiday makers, but everyone except for George manages to have fun in the sun. Charles Grodin plays George Lollar, and was the main star of the movie. Bud recalls an unusual responsibility. The production company had rented a seashore cottage for Mr. Grodin and Bud would take a speedboat every morning to pick up Mr. Grodin and get him to the set in time for his first scene. Christopher Ames played his brother, Brad, and Brenda Blake took the role of Veroneeka, supported by a large but relatively unknown cast.

Bud and Ron set up a tent for a base of operations for the movie that contained the black powder and all the needed equipment for explosions called for in the story. It also served as a bar and party tent for the cast and crew when work was done. They were almost finished with the production of "Resort" when Bud got a call from a Director, Paul Lynch, from 20th Century Fox to come immediately to British Columbia and be his Second Unit Director on a movie there. Ron Coe agreed to finish the work on "Resort," and Bud left for Canada with a quick stop at his home in Reseda, California. As you can imagine, Cowboy Bud's work life was intense. He was happy about his increased recognition for his talents but family life was spotty at best. A kiss "hello" and "goodbye" and he was gone again.

Bullies — 20th Century Fox

Paul Lynch directed this story of a peaceful family who moved into a small town in British Columbia, purchased a grocery store, and almost immediately were confronted by the Cullen family who had been bullying the town-folk for years. The Morris family becomes even more targeted when son Matt meets and likes Becky, who is a Cullen. She returns the affection which drives the conflict to brutal bullying and vicious assaults.

Several events caused a major change in the production schedule, the main one being the Director, Paul Lynch, got drunk and fell over a cliff. For two weeks Bud directed "Bullies" while Paul healed from a head wound.

The main location was at an Animal Farm. Although many animals were on the farm, sheep were prevalent. Their familiar bleating, "Baaaa," was often heard by the cast and crew while working on the movie. Some of the gals started rousting our Cowboy Bud saying, "They are calling you, Buuuuud!" Keeping life on the light side, Cowboy Bud bought about five pairs of rubber boots, placed them where all could see with a sign, "Rubber Boots for rent — 50 cents." Those of you that don't know, among country people, an old joke was if you put the back legs of a sheep in rubber boots, they could not get away from the shepherd boy. It was one way the goal of keeping life on the light side was achieved by "Buuuuud."

When the movie was finished, the usual 'Wrap Party' was held and the gals from the crew presented Cowboy Bud with a golden ram's head with an inscription, "To the great Buuuuud!"

Bud, as Second Unit Director on the movie and for a while, Director, allowed him to cover all the action sequences, his favorite part of movie-making. Not that he couldn't direct a love scene, and in the later years did on many movies, but his main background and experience was with, "Action!" — Therefore, the title of his biography.

Chapter Eleven
More Highlights — Movies and Television

As one of the pioneers of independent production in Hollywood, Cowboy Bud Cardos will go down in history as a leader and innovator both in front of the camera and as a creator of streamlined, lower budget movies behind the camera.

In the decades before the 1960s, seven major studios ruled the film capital of the world. They were MGM Studios, Paramount, Universal, Warner Brothers, Columbia, RKO and Republic Pictures where almost all of the early Westerns were made. Today, just about every production is a combination of independent financing and creative people. Bud became a working member of that core group that ended up changing motion picture production forever.

One of Bud's qualities was not to turn down work of any kind. In, "Run Home Slow," he worked as the Unit Production Manager and Stunt Gaffer (Director) an independent production starring Mercedes McCambridge, Linda Scott and Gary Kent with a strong supporting cast including Bud.

Mercedes succeeds in the role of Nell Hagen who sets out to retaliate for the hanging of her father Judd, who ruled their valley with an iron hand before the natives revolted. She is accompanied by her brothers, Ritt (Gary Kent) and Kirby, (Allen Richards) a hump-backed half-wit, and their sensuous cousin, Julie Ann (Linda Scott) who marries Ritt but gets naked and seduces Kirby. The family then robs a bank and kills two tellers before dropping in on Charley Gately, leader of the group that hung old man Hagen, killing him, his son Gabe and daughter-in-law, Ruth. They head for the border where it gets really mean and nasty.

A fight between Bud's character and Gary Kent as 'Ritt,' begins a long friendship between the two men and was a high point of the movie. They remain close friends to this day. In 2013, a series of their collective stunts with three other honored stuntmen were edited together. In Gary's hometown of Austin, Texas, each man was interviewed separately on a stage before a full house in a local theater after the red carpet greeting by TV, press and fans. One of the highlights for Cowboy Bud's interview was a film clip from the fight scene between Bud as Indian Chief, Satago, and myself as Ben Thompson, in the tag sequence of the Western, "Five Bloody Graves." Then, "Kingdom Of The Spiders," directed by Bud, was mentioned. He received a standing ovation from the packed theater audience.

Advertised around the country as, "Fantastic Film Festival," fans from all over the country attended. After each man was honored and over thirty minutes of autograph-signing in the theater, they all moved to the parking lot where several car 'gags' were performed; fiery, roll-over car crashes and high falls from the top of the theater's roof was presented by stunt 'gaffer', Bob Ivy.

The second day began with a local radio DJ dedicating a full hour to Bud and Gary remembering and recounting their work together and individually with the radio audience asking questions. It went so well a half-hour was added. The four day event included radio interviews, press and TV and was one of Cowboy Bud's gratifying memories of his career. The Film Commission of Texas sponsored a closing dinner for the stuntmen of Hollywood and everything during the entire stay was complimentary to Cowboy Bud and friends; all free. A bottle of Bud's favorite booze, Jim Beam, was at Bud's place at the table for the honored guest. Anything on the menu of the five-star Hotel was available. The dinner started at eight-thirty and management had to ask all to leave at midnight. The festival was a huge success. Appreciation from the public is always the best reward for years of work.

The first time Bud worked with Dick Clark, was in the production of "Psych-Out." The movie had a strong cast. Susan Strasberg, Jack Nickolson, Bruce Dern, Dean Stockwell and Bud, in a powerful story. Jenny (Susan Strasberg) a deaf runaway who has just arrived in San Francisco's Haight-Ashbury District to find her long-lost brother, a mysterious bearded sculptor known around town as, The Seeker. She falls in with a psychedelic band, Mumblin' Jim, whose members include Stoney (Jack Nickolson) Ben, and Elwood. They hide her from the fuzz (cops) in their crash pad, a Victorian house crowded with love beads and necking couples. Mumblin' Jim's truth-seeking friend Dave considers the band's pursuit of success "playing games," but he agrees to help Jennie anyway. The 'duo' of Cowboy Bud and Gary Kent as, "the thugs," again add their stunts and coordinated fight scenes to the action sequences.

At this point in Bud's career he also worked as an actor on TV shows like "Mannix," a long running TV series in its day starring Mike Connors. Bud went as a sound-man with Mr. Connors to Colorado for the World Premiere of the 1966 version of "Stagecoach," and also on one of the Academy Awards with Bob Hope. Bud supplied thirty parakeets for the Bobby Darin – Sandra Dee movie "If a Man Answers," a job offered by his animal wrangler friend, Jim Donaldson. He supplied the mocking bird for "To Kill a Mockingbird," one of Gregory Peck's great performances and the scorpion for "The Manchurian Candidate," starring Frank Sinatra, all giving you an idea of the diverse variety of Cowboy Bud's work.

One of his highest compliments came from Janet Leigh on a very different type of production called, "The Body Guard." It was shot with no-sync sound. All dialogue was off-camera; a very successful promo film with Janet Leigh presenting the concept of no-sync dialogue. She gave a high compliment to Bud for his directing, "His work as a director is like, Alfred Hitchcock — really exceptional."

During this period of independent producers with low budgets, Director/Producer Al Adamson came on the Hollywood scene, a guy who became known for his unusual productions through the years. Cowboy Bud first worked with Al on, "Blood Of Dracula's Castle." It was one of Al's first low budget movies as a Director, with a cast that included Alex De'Arcy, Paula Raymond, John Carradine, Bud, myself, and others; a good little movie. It has been mentioned in the chapter on stunts that it was a well-padded Bud doubling John Carradine taking a ten foot fall onto the cellar floor of Dracula's Castle causing the death of Carradine's character.

Al Adamson's, "The Female Bunch," has a pretty decent cast, headed by Lon Chaney, Jr. and Russ Tamblyn, the story line was after a string of bad times with men, Sandy (Nesa Renet) tries to kill herself. Co-waitress Libby (Rigina Carrol — later Al's wife) saves her and takes her to meet some female friends of hers who live on a ranch in the desert. Grace (Jennifer Bishop), the leader of the gang, puts Sandy through her initiation and they get on with the real job of running drugs across the Mexican border, hassling poor farmers, and taking any man they please; one being Bud as a Mexican farmer. They hung him from a tree wrapped in barbed-wire and then dragged him down a dirt road.

Bud being dragged in dirt — The Female Bunch

Brutal stuff! Soon Sandy becomes unsure if this is the life for her, but it may be too late to get out. Bud's role was small but pivotal in the story. The Western, "Five Bloody Graves," "Hell's Bloody Devils," and "Satan Sadists," to mention a few of the low budget movies directed by Al Adamson, each having very different, dimensional back stories.

An example of another Cardos stunt was the use of his 182 Cessna making a "blind landing" for Al when the story called for the leading lady to land the plane on a dirt airstrip and then taxi down a dirt road and park the plane in the back of a motel. How was it done? Bud flew the plane lying on the floor of the cockpit peeking through a crack in the plane's structure widened for the landing. Bud gave instructions to the actress from the floor on what to do and when. He operated the brakes. On the screen it looks like the girl is landing in full control of the aircraft.

182 Cessna

In between stunts and special effects, Bud worked different productions like, "The Birds," for Alfred Hitchcock. The order was, "Get birds! Lots of birds!" Cowboy Bud became the "bird wrangler" of Reseda, CA. At night and due to his background as an animal and bird man, he would go out to the local neighbor intersections. With a long pole at one end of the street-signs and a net at the other, he would poke the birds into the net.

All went well until one night Bud noticed a police car following him, intersection to intersection with its lights out. Finally one night they pulled up and had to ask, "What in the world are you doing?" Bud honestly replied, "Catching birds for a movie." You can imagine two cops looking at each other with wonder. Actually this kind of unusual behavior is common to the movie business and as usual what could Bud do or say. He shrugged his shoulders and told the cops, "It's a true story," with a smile. One of the cops became a close friend of Bud's, Paul Hospitar. He also wrote a column for the newspaper, The Valley Green Sheet. Paul reported the valley's own, Cowboy Bud Cardos, and all his future work in the movie industry.

Sandra Dee, Dean Stockwell, Ed Bagley starred in, "Dunwich Horror," with a well-known, good supporting cast. Bud helped cover an old house in Northern California with vines for a needed sequence working with a full union crew. His panel-truck with the road runner being chased by Wiley Coyote silk screened on the side of the truck with bold letters saying, "Run-a-way Productions." It raised some eyebrows and comments from the union crew but taken in good humor. As a matter of fact, the union guys were happy to have 'Run-a-way Cardos' around when they got stuck in the mud. Bud pulled them out with the wench on the front of his truck.

An added touch called for in the story, Bud provided an owl for the needed scenes and was the Art Director and special effects man helped by both Forest and Ron, his longtime co-workers. In the story, Dr. Henry Armitage, Sandra Dee and another girl who wasn't in the book, visit the library of the Miskatonic University where they are studying, and find a mysterious young man named Wilbur Whateley trying to borrow the Necronomicon (to non-HPL fans: a book containing ancient rites to bring alien gods to our planet), and as it is a public library they let him. Sandra Dee offers to drive the mustachioed warlock back to his home in Dunwich, where he drugs her and makes her stay to be a part in his evil ceremonies. As an aside, it was Bud's work as the Art Director in this movie that caused the union to call him in for a test to become a member. It is that test that revealed Cowboy Bud was color-blind! Oh well....

Then, "Nightmare In Wax." A story about a disfigured curator of a wax museum who murders his enemies and then uses their bodies as exhibits in his museum starring Cameron Mitchell, Scott Brady and Ann Helm. Bud played a part as an actor playing a cop and did stunts. One already mentioned, a fire stunt where Bud doubled Cameron Mitchell getting brandy splashed in his face. Cut: Bud steps up and in an over-shoulder shot on Barry who lights the brandy with a match and Bud spins low and on fire, goes crashing through sliding glass doors into a swimming pool.

The independent movie entitled, "Jud," gained acclaim for a car chase created by Cowboy Bud and was the beginning of a long relationship with Producer, Igo Kantor. The critics compared it to a famous car chase in the movie, "Bullet," starring Steve McQueen, being pursued at high speeds and sometimes leaving the ground, up and down the streets of San Francisco ending in a fiery crash. The Cardos car chase was shot on Sunset Boulevard at night through the Hollywood Hills. It is sequences like the Cardos chase that creates the best advertisement for a movie; word of mouth, one person telling another.

In "If A Man Answers," starring Sandra Dee and Bobby Darin. The story line: A rich socialite, Chantal, marries Eugene, a photographer and everything seems blissful until her envious friend attempts to break them up. In desperation, she turns to her mother, but the advice she receives may do more harm than good. This is the movie Bud supplied thirty parakeets and Bud performed numerous car stunts.

Another independent production, "The Incredible 2 headed Transplant," Bud was Second Unit Director, in charge of creating and filming the action sequences called for in the screenplay, plus he was the Unit Production Manager and did the special effects. The weird story of Dr. Roger Girard as a rich scientist conducting experiments on head transplantation. His caretaker has a son, Danny, who, although fully grown, has the mind of child. One day an escaped psycho-killer invades Girard's home, killing Danny's father before being gunned down himself.

With the maniac dying and Danny deeply unsettled by his father's death, Dr. Girard decides to take the final step and transplant the killer's head onto Danny's body. Of course, things go horribly wrong and the two-headed creature escapes to terrorize the countryside.

The movie starred, Bruce Dern, Casey Kasem, and Pat Priest. A strong supporting cast gave the movie some frightening moments helped by Bud's exceptional special effects. He made a trip to the San Diego Zoo where there were housed some actual two-headed animals; a king snake with two heads, a two-headed monkey and a pig. He took film footage of the freaks of nature and brought it back to Hollywood.

Next was, "The Werewolf Of Woodstock," for Dick Clark Productions (a movie of the week). Dick became one of Bud's closest, personal friends in life. Cowboy Bud was the werewolf and did a very exceptional job of scaring audiences world-wide in his wolf-man, hairy costume. Bud and stuntman Bobby Clark staged a sensational fight scene ending with "Werewolf Bud" crashing through a door; dead.

Bobby Clark and Bud as Werewolf

His make-up call was three in the morning to be ready by six-thirty and eating was through a straw. One scene Bud will always remember was running up a flight of stairs carrying the leading lady, a stunt demanding leg strength had by few.

It was behind the scenes that the bond of friendship continued to develop with Dick Clark. For those of you that don't know, Mr. Clark had a most successful, teenage TV song and dance program called, "American Bandstand," for many years and until shortly before his death, Americans and people all over the world, saw Dick Clark doing the count-down as the ball dropped in Times Square in New York City every New Year's Eve celebrating the New Year. I will share more about Bud and Dick Clark later in a chapter, "Dick and Me."

Bud took the job of Second Unit Director on "House Of Terror" — the title reveals the story line. Jennifer Andrews (Jennifer Bishop) arrives at a forbidding house in the Hollywood Hills, as she is the new nurse hired by an extremely rich man, Emmett Kramer (Mitchell Gregg) to minister to his whining, neurotic, bedridden wife, Marsha (Jacqueline Hyde). Mark Alden (Arell Blanton) Jennifer's former lover before he was sent to prison, shows up hoping his animal magnetism will rekindle their old affair. Jennifer manages to attend to her shrewish patient professionally, thereby earning the gratitude of the husband. His gratitude soon turns to love. When the suicidal inclined Marsha is found dead in her blood-smeared bathroom, he is free to marry Jennifer. Mark, who has perfected the art of getting everything for nothing, sees the marriage as an opportunity to get his hands on Kramer's fortune, by planning an "accidental" death for him. Then the dead wife's twin sister, Dolores Beaudine arrives and quickly uncovers Mark's scheme and deals herself in on it.

Director Oliver Drake approached our independent production team wanting to produce a screenplay written by him, "No Tears For The Damned." I played the male lead and Bud arranged the stunts and special effects. The movie was also released under the title of "The Vegas Strangler." We shot most of the movie in Las Vegas with some scenes shot at a ranch house about one hundred miles from Las Vegas. From the title you know my character (Jeff) was a killer, sick in the head from a domineering mother, who gave her son an impression of other women as evil. His sickness manifested in an uncontrollable desire to kill beautiful show girls — which he did. Not a great movie but a good, low budget action movie. Bud was in charge of stunts and special effects.

Sometimes, the story behind the scenes stay with us longer than the plot of the movie. Bud needed to put bubble bath in the indoor pool in a suite used by us at the Riviera Hotel to cover for the nakedness of one of Jeff's victims. He had bubbles half as high as the ceiling. What management forgot to tell us was that our pool and its systems were connected to the other suites in that wing of the Hotel. Bubbles and more bubbles filled all of the adjoining suites making the hotel guests very unhappy, particularly the romantic couples. What could we say, "That's show-biz," and arranged for cleaning up the mess.

"Country A-Go-Go," a TV series showcased the biggest names in the music world and is mostly lost to history but it was produced by one of the most interesting characters to ever appear behind the scenes in Hollywood, Al Ganaway. "Country" had more than forty stars like Merle Haggard, Marty Robbins and the list goes on and on. Al ended up with the nick name of "Run-away-Ganaway." When he whipped out his gold pen, beware!

Bud was the Unit Production Manager on "Country." He found an old warehouse on the outskirts of Las Vegas and transformed it into a sound stage where the segments with the many recording and movie stars, came to add their talent. Ganaway had the ability to promote big stars to work for him and as Bud recalls on the "Country A-Go-Go" series. The biggest challenge for Cowboy Bud was getting needed monies for production expenses. Al would crack open the door to his suite and stick cash out through the opening. The plus for Bud from the work was meeting the stars, many who became long-time friends.

"Savage Seven," — a good action movie starring, Adam Roarke, Robert Walker, Jr., Joanna Frank, John Garwood and Cowboy Bud as, "Running Buck." The story line was about a biker gang leader Kisum (Adam Roarke) who loves waitress Marcia Little Hawk (Joanna Frank). Her brother Johnnie Little Hawk (Robert Walker, Jr.), the leader of a group of American Indians disapproves. At various times these two groups are adversaries and allies. The two groups join forces but crooked businessmen scheme to have them at each other's throats again. The theme song "Anyone for Tennis" is by Cream. "The Iron Butterfly" is heard playing their classic "Iron Butterfly Theme." Producer Dick Clark and director Richard Rush had made "Psych-Out" earlier in the year. It helped the growing respect and friendship between Bud and Dick Clark.

This is the movie where Bud, while riding on horseback, created a stunt where he gets knocked off his horse by a member of the motorcycle gang. He was pinned down under a motorcycle. The engine kept running, and in gear, grinding flesh from Bud's stomach with the back tire being the knobby off-road type. Remember, Bud had to keep his head down and take the grinding on his belly. If he jumped up from the pain, he could have been killed by motorcycles flying overhead.

Bud was Second Unit Director on, "Won Ton Ton: The Dog That Saved Hollywood," starring, to mention a few but not all of the stars, Terri Garr, Bruce Dern, Dorothy Lamore, Ann Miller, Andy Devine, Johnny Wisemuller, Art Carney and just about every star in Hollywood! The story: In 1924, Estie comes to Hollywood to become an actress but the dog that followed her becomes the star. Hollywood has its own rules for success. Obviously, "Won Ton Ton" is a situation comedy that did very well at the box-office with the help of the big name movie stars, many who got to know Cowboy Bud and looked forward to working with him again.

Bud recalls lunch dates with Director, Michael Winner, a character in his own right. A man with plenty of personal wealth enjoyed having lunch with golden goblets and all the amenities and service of a king. In his own mind he was. A good point to remember: any clash between a king and a cowboy, bet on the cowboy. Bud knowing how to indirectly direct, got along fine with, "the king."

Here was a man who wrote his own epitaph recognizing his lack of popularity by adding, "Someone will probably drop a 10K (a motion picture, cast iron light) on my head!" The star, Marlon Brando, peed on Michael from high in the catwalks of a sound stage demonstrating his displeasure of him as a Director!

After "Won Ton Ton," one day Bud got an urgent call from his UPM friend (Unit Production Manager) Paul, "Get to Chicago ASAP!" He needed help and a plane ticket was waiting for Bud. Come quick! Bud was working in the warmth of Nevada. He packed his suitcase and headed for the airport in time to catch the next plane to Chicago. Landing at O'Hare Airport, the greeting from the stewardess to Mr. Cardos was, "Welcome to Chicago. It is eight degrees above zero." By the time Bud got to his hotel he was cold to the bone beneath his light shirt and sweater. He remembers sitting in the warm water of the bathtub in his room with a bottle of Jim Beam whiskey trying to get warm!

After helping Paul with a couple of car crashes and doubling Larry Starch in a hanging scene, Bud went home to California swearing to, "Never go back!" He had been home a couple of days and he got another call from Paul, "Come back!" Honoring his own code, "Money talks and bullshit walks," Bud immediately went to his neighborhood wilderness store and bought enough warm clothes to make a movie at the North Pole!

It is good to mention the "Wrap Parties" at the Cardos residence. They were unique to say the least. From a friend in the restaurant supply business, an order for one of Bud's pool parties was sixty-five pounds of chicken, twenty pounds of hamburger, one-half gallon of Bourbon, scotch and vodka, ten cases of beer and ten cases of soda pop. In addition, people would bring more food and booze.

A "Mime" in white-face (he does not blink!) was by the sliding glass door to the pool. Girls would try to get him to move or blink. Convinced he was a statue, one girl turned her back, got pinched in the butt by the mime and jumped into the pool! Good times for families and friends. Caesar Romero would give his crazy laugh from "The Joker" for the kids and people would come and go by the hundreds in an afternoon and evening.

They were the best parties including the fireworks on the Fourth of July. Cowboy Bud was a knowledgeable "powder monkey," buckets would be blown a hundred feet in the air with all the neighbor friends with their kids lining the street and front yards enjoying the fireworks.

Up to four hundred people signed the guest book for one of many Cardos pool parties.

Drinks at the bar by the pool and music heard through the professional sound system. Cowboy Bud would even pick up his guitar and sing some of his songs from his 'pickin' and singin' in the saloons in his younger days. All were friends from the motion picture profession; stars, their friends, families, crew members and neighbors included. Many good times!

Jack Palance and Script Supervisor, Karen

Bud, Patty & Caesar Ramero

After about 10 years of the loved Cardos parties, a neighbor moved in across the street with wild gatherings, playing loud 'heavy metal', a noise they called music. All kinds of drugs and bad behavior caused the cops to show up with a SWAT Team to break it up. The Cardos friendly-family-and-friends parties were never the same as arrests across the street continued and ruined the happy times for the whole neighborhood.

Chapter Twelve
Cowboy Bud — Animal Man

Bud has a natural, spirit based connection with animals. It has always been part of who he is. As a young guy about six years old, he had a pet goat. He taught it primarily by just talking to it. The goat would follow him wherever he would go. The same with his first puppy, who was trained to jump into and wait patiently in a cardboard box on the back of the Bud's bicycle until his master returned from the market or any other destination. For sure food was used in the training of all Cardos animals through the years. He never whipped or beat an animal. Like the "Horse Whisperer," his main training tools were time and love creating a lasting bond.

Horses, Mules and Burros

We have already established that Cowboy Bud's first horse was his white mare, "Trouble." She was a wonderful companion providing days of saddle adventures for a young cowboy. She was from the stables in Big Bear, CA, and moved to San Gabriel and the Cardos family home there.

"Trouble" had a love affair with a stallion in Big Bear and after the normal eleven months, she had a foal, a stud, Bud named "Double Trouble," DT for short. Here, at birth, is where Cowboy Bud's instincts took over. Never having had training as a horse trainer, Bud implemented his own. From the day DT was born, Bud would pick the horse up in his arms and talk to him. He did this until DT got too heavy to lift off the ground. Then he would put DT's front feet on his shoulders, not a difficult task when he was a young colt but imagine a nine hundred pound fully grown horse on command running up to you, rearing up and putting his front hoofs on your shoulders! The "Wheelbarrow Trick" where Bud would pick up the horse's back feet and wheel him around until the colt became a horse and too heavy. DT and Bud did tricks no professional trainer had thought of. Again, the Cardos way — he thought it up and just did it.

Bud with DT

Life with DT was colorful to say the least. Their young years were spent together in both Big Bear and San Gabriel and later in the horse arena clowning together. For example, DT was trained not to respond to a rider on his back in the center of the arena during one of Bud's clowning acts. With all kinds of urging from the rider, DT would just stand there, so the announcer would say, "There is something wrong with this horse! Is there a doctor in the house?!"

This was Cowboy Bud's cue to come out of the stands dressed in his clown pants, white coat and hat with his doctor's bag, and run to the center of the arena, getting the horse to lie down. He would pull a large bumper-jack out of his bag and proceed to jack-up DT's rear leg in a sling at the end of the jack. As "The Doc," Bud started exaggeratingly pumping on an eight-foot handle as the horse's leg would rise up. Next, Doc pulled out a blanket and threw it over the horse and ducked under it, first throwing out some chickens, then pigeons and lastly a small pig which would run squealing around the arena. Lastly, DT was released from the jack; got up and both men would climb on board. On command, DT would take off! DT would run around the arena and Bud would roll backwards and grabbing DT's tail, proceed to ski behind the horse. The crowds loved it!

Another clowning gag was Bud riding into the arena on the back of a burro playing a loud version of the Elvis hit song, "Hound Dog." He had black powder in the hollow of the guitar and on cue it would blow-up. When the smoke cleared, the sad clown would be sitting on the fence with the broken guitar dangling down.

DT and Bud had a relationship rarely seen between a man and his horse. Bud could take a nap using DT for a pillow. The horse was completely harmless around children and they loved him. Bud and DT always won first place in local "Gym-Cannas" (competitive horse and rider events). Their favorite event was where all the competitor's saddles are piled up in the center of the arena. The horses are turned lose. On the starter's gun, the idea was to catch your horse, find your saddle in the pile and saddle your horse and dash to the finish line. As you would expect, it was a scramble with people chasing their horses, catching them, finding their saddle then putting the saddle and bridle on the horse, and dashing for the finish line.

At the starter's gun, Cowboy Bud would walk to the center of the arena while all the other competitors ran for their horses. Bud would first get his saddle and bridle and then whistle for DT who would trot over to him. A time-saver was Bud did not have to totally cinch up the saddle on DT's back. He would put one loop through the d-ring at the end of the webbing and pull it snug. Then would wrap the latigo around the saddle horn, jump on DT and make it to the finish line. No one ever beat them.

On a pleasure ride one time a group of riders came to a seven foot drop-off. The group decided they had to go the long way around. Not Cowboy Bud and DT. Bud took the saddle off and had DT lie down with his feet towards Bud. He pushed DT off the small cliff. DT rolled over and landed on his feet. Man and horse were waiting for the other riders when they showed up some time later. "Now how did you do that, Bud?" Bud responded with his usual smile.

An annual event called, Old Miner's Race, was unusual to say the least. It entailed one hundred wild burros rounded up and corralled in Apple Valley, CA, a community at the base of the San Bernardino Mountains, seven thousand feet below Big Bear. Bud would make simple pack-saddles for the animal's backs consisting of a small, split log and belly strap. At the start of the race, people from all walks of life, mostly a little worse for wear, from partying all night, would get a hold of a burro's lead rope and start the trek up the mountain. The scramble was always fun and humorous. They would stumble and fumble pulling not very cooperative burros, some breaking away heading back out into the high desert.

Bud and DT with a trailer had the job of rounding up the strays that got away. Bud would throw a rope on the wild burro, get him to the back of the trailer then run the rope through the front slats of the trailer, hook it up to DT's saddle and the horse would pull the burro into the trailer for transport. If the burro resisted, DT would just drag him in. One time Bud was swatting a burro on the butt trying to help DT get the animal in the trailer and a car full of young girls who had been partying all day and probably the night before stopped and one girl yelled, "Stop beating that poor animal!" Bud's said, looking over his shoulder "You're next, lady!" and added the Cardos' smile. The girls screamed and sped away. The second day of the race was up the mountain and the third day was making it to the finish line in Big Bear. A good time was had by all.

DT had a stable-mate, "Fuego" ("Fire" in Spanish) a Palomino Mare and another of Bud's really good, saddle horses. Quick footed and to the rein, only an accomplished rider was allowed to ride her. She won many blue ribbons and different competitions. DT's mother, "Trouble" passed on after a good life spending her last year in San Gabriel. The years Bud spent in Big Bear were mostly with his horses, family and friends. To this day on the Cardos, "Wild Sage Canyon Ranch," where he shares ownership with his long-time, trusted friend, 'Letty,' the animal population includes; "Ludie Mae," (Bud's mule who won the 300 yard dash in nineteen seconds — 1988 at Los Alamitos, CA — a track record) she is still a star in the Mule Racing Community. Her retirement today at the Wild Sage Canyon Ranch is much deserved. She always supported herself with being in the money over ninety percent of her racing life. She was self-supporting and more at race tracks like Ruidoso, New Mexico, Winnemucca, Nevada, and others. Bud and his Cowboy & Mule buddies would drive or fly to the Mule Races and enjoy the Star, 'Ludie Mae'.

Ludie Mae

At Cowboy Bud's Wild Sage Canyon Ranch, lives his buffalo named, "Buffy" and Bud's grand-daughter, Ariel's horse whose named is "Buck." Then there was "Quincy Blue," a horse Bud says along with DT were two horses that were 'Nearly perfect'. DT and Quincy Blue, are now in horse heaven but were in the family for a long time. Quincy Blue would come when hearing Bud's whistle and slide to a stop at his feet. A mare named, "Beauty," aging and more of a pet and stable mate. Also, another of Ariel's horses, "Jada," an Albino (white) horse with stark blue eyes.

Quincy Blue

The "Wild Sage Canyon Ranch" is a work in progress with something new always being added including better facilities for boarding horses. It takes many working hours to maintain any operation that includes such a variety of God's creatures but it seems to have always been in Cowboy Bud's blood, to love and care for animals. He loves them and they love him.

When Bud and his first wife, Barbara, agreed to disagree in Big Bear, the separation broke Bud's bank and if you remember from his earlier life, Bud went to Las Vegas with ten cents in his pocket and a tank of gas in an old pick-up truck rigged for both gas and propane. Bud made arrangements with the stable and a good friend there to take care of DT. The friend assured Bud he would be well cared for and that was the parting of two very close pals.

As the saying goes, "Bud went down the road of life." The man had to part from his horse he loved with all his heart.

Dogs and Other Good Friends

Cowboy Bud's life story would not be complete without mentioning at least some of the other good friends. Some you may recall the Gibbon Ape, Freddy Cardos, who co-starred with Bud during his clowning years at rodeos after he received his wings from the infamous flight as a passenger on PSA Airlines. Diane, the lioness, who worked the Las Vegas Strip with Bud and friends in his younger years including the variety of animals bought from Mexico to work in movies.

Dogs have been a big part of Bud's life through the years. A recent heart-break for Bud was the loss of his dog, K-Bar, to cancer. It is really hard to put the love and affection for one dog above the other. The love is for all but different for each one. More than a pet they are a buddy, a friend and in most of Bud's life, a constant companion. K-Bar, a Border Collie, was highly intelligent and an ever-present partner with Cowboy Bud. He was very well trained by voice commands and completely obedient. He was given to Bud by his life-long friend, Elliot, a rancher in Wyoming who recently died very close to K-Bar's passing, a coincident that gives us a pause to reflect on The Creator of all life.

K-Bar

From early years Bud had a dog and at times, lots of dogs. You may recall the summers in Big Bear in the High School years. Bud and his buddies would camp in tents outside the Cardos Cabin because Mr. Cardos, Sr., and friends were inside. The guys decided to get a watch-dog to guard them and their property in their tent complex. From the dog-pound they got a big and as advertised, a mean, German shepherd that was to be put down because no one would adopt him. They named him, "Capp," and he lived up to his reputation. The guys put Capp on a twenty-foot chain tied to a tree. To get into their own tents, one guy would distract the snapping, snarling, growling Capp by running in one direction while others would run for their tent. With the Cardos touch, Capp was eventually trained and tamed but remained a good watch-dog.

Of course, Cowboy Bud had his horse, DT. His friends from school, before going up to Big Bear for a summer, would buy a horse. They could get a good saddle-broke horse for fifty dollars. They would trailer the horses up to Big Bear, with the horses their only form of transportation for the summer, while they all found work around the stables, hotels and local businesses. It was a life they really enjoyed.

Capp went with Bud back to San Gabriel after summer-time. He became a good member of the Cardos family, a family that included a three-legged female Shepherd, "Sam," deserving of additional mention as a most unusual pal and pet.

When Bud was working on the movie, "Won Ton Ton," the dog that saved Hollywood, the star-dog, a German Shepherd, was a highly intelligent, well trained dog. There is always a 'glitch' when working with animals, the unforeseen problem with what appears as a simple piece of action, a scene where "Won Ton Ton" was to show his distaste for a particular character and pee on the guy's leg. All kinds of coaxing didn't work so finally Bud and some other crew members peed into bottles and took turns 'baiting the trousers' with scent. Finally the star-dog peed on the guy's leg and they got it on film — to much applause!

By the end of the movie, Bud and the star-dog had bonded as buddies. The owner-trainer with thanks and understanding of Bud's affection for star-dog, gifted him with a female from a litter star-dog had fathered; a beautiful, female Shepherd puppy Bud named, "Samantha," which was shortened to, "Sam." They went everywhere together. When Sam got older one of their adventures was to fly in Bud's plane up to Bud's cabin in the High Sierras in a little community known as, Kennedy Meadows.

One trip turned out to be bad luck for Sam when she jumped out of Bud's Dune Buggy and was run-over. The back tire ruined Sam's left front leg. It had to be amputated. As Bud recalls her amazing spirit, "You would not believe her recovery. It seemed just a short time and she was chasing rabbits moving deftly with only one leg in front."

From Sam's first litter, Bud kept the biggest pup and named him, "Jim Beam." Both mother and son had a long life in the Cardos home although long gone, the memories of the good life are recalled often when Cowboy Bud reaches for his favorite beverage, Jim Beam, still in first position at the Cardos bar!

Through the years there was, "Pal," who died on an operating table, accidentally killed by an inept veterinarian; "Romeo" who was very popular with all female dogs. Later with wife, Barbara, in Big Bear; sixteen hunting dogs used by Bud for bear hunting. His main hunting dog was fearless, named "Wrangler." One day a bear was cornered in a shallow cave and fearless Wrangler went after him. It was his last fearless move. Death becomes part of owning animals and a constant part of life. The feeding, caring and training is time consuming. Bud put it this way, "I know it was a big part of the break-up with Barbara."

An Airedale named "Rusty" (named because of his color) was a Cardos dog. Not only a family pet but a movie dog as well. Highly intelligent and always responsive to Bud's voice commands. There was one exception when instinct superseded obedience. On the set of Arch Hall's, "Deadwood 76," like on all movie sets, Rusty was trained by Bud to stay behind the camera. No matter what the action was going on before the camera, Rusty stayed out of the scenes. However, the one exception came to light during a scene where actor Jack Lester was selling cats to a group of townspeople as "mousers" for their barns. In a flash, Rusty burst into the scene and started killing cats, right and left, tossing them in the air and chasing them around the western street. Before Bud could get a hand on him, all had been sent to kitty heaven. What could Cowboy Bud do but go back to the animal control facility and get more cats to complete the scene?

In "Blood of Dracula's Castle," Rusty was the lead tracking-dog, when I as "Crazy Johnny" escaped from an Insane Asylum by paying off a guard (played by Bud) to open the gate. I beat the guard to death with his own gun and made a run for freedom.

We took Rusty to Manzanillo, Mexico, when as, "Contigo Productions," we produced my original screenplay, "The Greatest Treasure." The malfunction of our sound camera caused all our sound sequences to be in soft focus, so the whole effort was a heart-breaker. The movie was never completed for the silver screen. The adventure was unforgettable for our cast and crew, including Rusty. One of the memorable moments was the transfer of Rusty (while in the plywood cage Bud had built for the trip) was moved from the big jet we took from Los Angeles to Guadalajara, Mexico, to the smaller DC-3 for the short trip to Manzanillo. A Mexican man only about five-foot three inches at most, picked up the plywood cage with

Rusty (who weighed about 75 lbs.) inside, with great effort started the trek for the smaller aircraft. All of us, cast and crew, watched as the little guy would have to move one way and then the other as Rusty would move from one side of the cage to the other. When he made it to the DC-3, we all gave him a round of applause for his mighty, successful effort. It should be noted there were fewer cats in Mexico when we left!

There was, "Jimmy," the raccoon (who most of the time, lived in his cage Bud built for him, next to the pool area in the Cardos backyard). Jimmy worked in movies, too. On, "Killers Three," filmed in the Southern States, Bud and Jimmy stayed in a local Holiday Inn. On one occasion when Bud had to go to work without Jimmy, he locked the raccoon in the bathroom and put the "Do Not Disturb" sign on the door-knob.

Bud and Jimmy, the raccoon

When Bud got back to the room after work, he opened the bathroom door to find not one little piece of wall-paper left on the wall! Jimmy had stripped it clean! Bud had his personal plane on that production and after checking the phone book and doing the necessary research, found the supplier for all Holiday Inns in the area. He and his assistant, Sue, flew to Raleigh,

North Carolina, got the matching wallpaper and flew back to the Holiday Inn. Bud made the bathroom look like new. The only problem was Bud threw the shreds of old wallpaper in the hotel's trash bin. When discovered, it was reported to the manager. The manager searched the hotel several times for the room missing the wallpaper. It was never found.

Chapter Thirteen
Dick and Me

There are some people that become special in our lives. So it was between Cowboy Bud and Dick Clark, the world famous personality from years of being on television with his teenage song and dance program called, "American Bandstand." Many singers began their careers on Dick's show with his support; to mention a few out of many, Frankie Avalon, Bobby Rydell, Fabian, Smokey Robinson and "The Supremes." The series remained popular for thirty years.

Expanding his horizons into Motion Picture Production, Mr. Clark signed a three picture deal with American International Pictures. Their first collective effort was a movie entitled, "Flower Children," starring Jack Nickleson. Bud's stuntman buddy, Gary Kent, called him for help with the stunts on the movie. It was on the set of this production; Bud was introduced to Dick Clark. The two men clicked from the beginning with Bud recalling, "He was a nice, regular guy."

The second Clark Production entitled, "Savage Seven," was filmed mostly in the little town of Nipton, CA. Directed by Richard Rush, starring Robert Walker Jr., Joanna Frank, John Garwood, and Larry Bishop. Biker gang leader Kisum (Adam Rourke) loves waitress Marcia Little Hawk. During production, Bud did his usual stunt-work including the one that ground a layer of flesh off of his stomach mentioned in chapter nine. During time between set-ups and the business of making a movie, Bud and Dick became more acquainted evolving to a closer relationship over drinks after work.

Bud began mentioning his work in the independent field of production and how production costs could be substantially reduced. Their mutual respect grew into a real friendship. In subsequent meetings, Dick learned of the truth Cowboy Bud shared and made him an official member of the Dick Clark production team by hiring Bud to do pre-production on his third movie for American International Pictures, "Killers Three," to star Dick Clark, Robert Walker Jr., Diane Varsi and Norman Alden.

Sight unseen, Cowboy Bud bought a Tri-Pacer airplane and had it delivered to the San Fernando Airport. His friend and Cardos Team member, Rick Jackson, who had no experience in small planes and with total trust in Bud as a pilot, climbed on board and they headed east. At the same time, Forrest Carpenter, Bud's long time co-worker, left his home in South Carolina in his GTO car. They rendezvoused in Chapel Hill, North Carolina. Bud had instructions from Dick to scout Chapel Hill where American International Pictures had just completed "Three In The Attic," for possible locations for, "Killers Three" and pick-up two Production Assistants, Sue Arnold and another, young 'PA' who's name has been lost in time. So the Cardos Team consisted of Cowboy Bud, Rick Jackson, Sue Arnold, Forrest Carpenter and the young man we will call, 'PA', for 'Production Assistant'.

Bud deemed Chapel Hill wrong for, "Killers Three." He left his Tri-Pacer airplane tied down at the airport in Chapel Hill. The Cardos Team piled into Forrest's car and started scouting different towns in the state. Sleeping in the car and eating canned food stopping only for bathroom breaks, they worked their way south through numerous small towns looking for one that would accommodate the storyline of the movie. Young 'PA' received an education in independent production away from the restraints of a full union crew and their rules and regulations. A comment remembered was, "Don't you guys ever sleep or stop to eat?"

The search continued investigating small towns hoping to meet the needs of the story. Several days of this grueling effort, the team came to Ramseur, NC, a town that provided an empty grocery store, bank and other needs for the production of the movie in a small town with one main street. Grubby Bud and Rick Jackson, both needing a bath and a shave walked into the local bank, Bud with his snap-brimmed hat and dark glasses hanging on his shirt pocket. The banker was concerned to say the least when Bud said he wanted to open an account and they were going to make a movie in his town.

The next morning when the banker received ten thousand dollars that was wired to him from Dick Clark giving Bud the power of the pen, the Banker welcomed a cleaned up Cowboy Bud. The Banker and Bud became good friends and he became most helpful to the Cardos Team. The man had an airstrip on his property he allowed Bud to use.

According to the screenplay for "Killers Three," Bud and his crew began preparing sets needed for the production of the movie to such an extent, that when the full union crew arrived to formally start pre-production, the work was done. The biggest accomplishment that caused Dick Clark to express amazement was the rental of the whole town signed and agreed to by the Mayor for two-hundred dollars!

By the time Dick Clark and his Location Manager arrived in Ramseur, Bud had accomplished much of the work including the stocking of the grocery store which was a 'set' for many scenes in, "Killers Three." "Rebel Yell" was a local whiskey in the area. Bud promoted two cases of pints of the booze. Dick Clark was playing an alcoholic, explosions expert, not a good combination. Bud supplied a fresh pint of Rebel Yell during the making of the movie. He called all the suppliers needed to stock the grocery store from soup to nuts. Bread was the only product Bud had to pay for. The rest he got for free from all the suppliers for advertising their products in the movie. The grocery store looked so real that people would try to do their marketing there.

Dick Clark sent Bud to one of his TV stations in Columbia, SC, to deliver an important message in person. When Bud returned in his plane he was met by Forest Carpenter telling him he had an appointment right away at the Hancock Hams to try and get meat for the grocery store. He took off coat and tie and they drove to the headquarters where the company was located and walked in the front door. There were two guys sitting, picking and singing country songs, one on a banjo and a less qualified guy on a guitar. Cowboy Bud and Forest listened and observed a while. "Howdy boys!" was the welcome. At a break, Bud asked if he could sit in. They invited him to join. Bud led them into some old favorites like, "Hey Good Looking," and others. They really got to rocking. One of the men pulled out a jug of whiskey from behind his chair. Little did Bud know that the man that was playing guitar and singing country songs with him was the owner of Hancock Hams. The outcome was the next day Hancock Hams supplied the total meat counter with different displays of meats and even decorative hams hanging from the ceiling in the grocery store.

Bud obtained from a furniture store next to the market an old safe. The story point regarding the safe involved Dick Clark as the alcoholic bad guy with Robert Walker, Jr.; was a scene where they were to blow up the safe while trying to rob the grocery store while Diane Varsi waited in the get-away car outside. Too much dynamite blew the safe through the store floor also alerting the sheriff played by the world renowned Country Singer, Merle Haggard.

The young 'PA' trying to impress Mr. Clark, went out and promoted twenty cases of Coke. When Bud found out what the assistant had done, he had to take him aside and explain that Mr. Clark had a large investment in Dr. Pepper and would not approve of promoting the competition in his movie. The young assistant learned the difficult lesson to ask questions before acting on his own and returned the cases of coke.

Bud's team was always close to being first in the morning dining hall of the hotel which looked out through large, glass windows onto the swimming pool and the five tiers of hotel rooms beyond. The morning's entertainment was watching the scene on the walkways across from the pool when just before the wake-up call was sent out, guys and girls partially dressed in their shorts and underwear and carrying clothes would be seen running back to their assigned rooms. Like musical chairs, it was musical rooms!

On the Labor Day break in principle photography, Dick and Bud were seated at a table having lunch when Paul Lewis, Production manager for American International Pictures, came up and asked, "Bud would you do something for me?" Dick interrupted and said, "I have something for Bud to do." Paul acknowledged the boss and left. As Dick and Bud were leaving the room, Dick stopped and shook Bud's hand leaving a gold American Express Card and said, "There is a first class, round trip ticket waiting for you. Go home and don't spare the expense."

Bud flew his Tri-Pacer to Charlotte, NC; about one hundred miles north of Ramseur, tied it down and caught a first class commercial flight to CA. He and his wife, Pat, "painted the town" every night in Los Angeles. An added piece of good news was Pat Cardos was pregnant with their fourth child. Bud had a great Labor Day vacation thanks to his friend, Dick Clark.

Making a movie always has many humorous and interesting activities behind the camera and like making a movie about making a movie, there are additional highlights behind the scenes worth sharing to give you an idea of "the Cardos way" of meeting production demands.

Like the sequence in the screenplay of "Killers Three," requiring an actual, backwoods, moonshine "still." Through the "good old boys" from Hancock Hams, Bud was introduced to a legitimate moonshiner, a man in his sixties who had lived a life of dodging the federal authorities in Ramseur. In fact the man had never had a Social Security number. By all known guidelines, he did not exist.

The social graces for a moonshine family was, besides drinking White Lighting that was guaranteed not to be over ninety days old, Bud soon became accepted having owned hunting dogs and been raccoon hunting as a younger man, getting invited to go coon-hunting with the moonshiner and his sons. The Cardos Team joined the hunt. However, Rick Jackson and Sue Arnold (having been given the nickname of "Huck," because of her attempts to be one of the boys) were not really able to meet the challenge. Hunting coons was part of Forest's life in the south, as well.

The hunt began and the moonshiner's two boys, both over six feet and true backwoods, young men and tough as nails, got liquored up on moonshine, ran after the five hounds in pursuit of a coon and at top speed hit unseen, three strands of barbed wire — "Twang!" They untangled themselves, ignored their wounds, jumped up, renewed their spirits with more White Lighting and continued the chase.

The dogs had treed the raccoon when the boys first arrived with Bud and Forest not far behind. A treed raccoon is not a happy animal and every time one of the boys tried to capture it, they would get knocked out of the tree. Bud could not help being amazed how the boys, one after another, would fall some twenty feet, bounce off the ground and immediately get up and go up the tree again. The raccoon was captured.

After the social outing with the Moonshiner and his family, Bud and Forest drove to Columbia, SC, and acquired a moonshine still needed for, "Killers Three." They loaded it on a rented, flatbed truck and headed back to Ramseur. As bad luck happens, two Southern cops pulled them over. When Bud explained the still was a prop for a movie, the cops finally understood why they were transporting such an illegal device. The Highway Patrol Cops strongly suggested to shoot some holes in the still while going through that part of the country and put a tarp over it! Bud politely agreed.

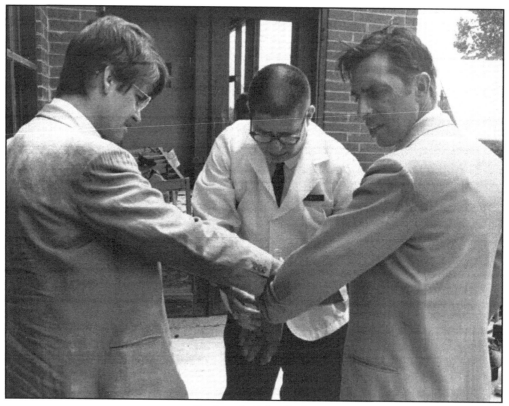

Bud and Dick Clark

A Hollywood crew in a small, southern town on a Sunday where recreational activities are very limited can be a problem for the management of the Holiday Inn there. Who knows how it starts but one Sunday a chair was tossed from one of the five floors that faced the swimming pool. Then a second and by evening time there was over fifty chairs in the pool.

Dick Clark accepted the crew "blowing off steam" and calmed the management. Another way Dick endeared himself to his crew. Their loyalty ran deep.

On another weekend, for diversion, Dick planned a big BBQ for the cast and crew. A problem arose. No grill for the BBQ. Bud went into town to find one, not paying attention to the fact it was Sunday and everything is closed except church in the bible-belt states. Frustrated, Bud looked high and low for someone to help him. Having no luck, he spotted an old refrigerator for sale in front of a store. One of the grills was marked fifty cents. With all good intentions to pay the money, he took the grill back to the party. Not long after his return, two cops showed up. They apparently saw Bud "steal" the grill. Starting to arrest him for his vile crime, Dick stepped in and long story short, prevented Bud from going to jail — just another day on location while making a movie.

One evening Dick approached Bud and said, "You never have seen the finished release print of, 'Savage Seven'. I had a print sent to me from Hollywood. I rented an RV (motor home) and made arrangements to screen it at the local drive-in after the last showing lets out at eleven." The guys arrived about an hour early and started having cocktails in the motor home while waiting for the main feature to conclude. In that hour both Dick and Bud got a little more than tipsy.

After the last car left the drive-in, they drove the motor home into a parking place, front and center, and the projectionist rolled the movie. Soon after main titles it started to rain. Not only did Dick fire up the engine and put on the windshield wipers but went out and started wiping the windshield with a rag. Eventually realizing and laughing at their plight, they had another drink and headed back to the Holiday Inn to see the movie some other time.

A young boy about nine years old played a role in "Killers Three." To show how pleased Dick was with the boy's performance, he asked Bud if he could find a pony and a saddle for the boy. It was to be presented as a "thank you" at a wrap party for the movie at the Holiday Inn's Convention Hall. Bud went on the hunt. Bud phone he found a saddle in a shop about thirty miles from town and flew his Tri-Pacer up to get it and returned but took some extensive searching for a pony. He finally found a pretty, brown and white pony but then transport became a problem. Bud solved it by putting the pony in the back seat of a passenger car and drove off with the pony's head sticking out of the back window.

Next came the problem of getting the pony to the Convention Room in time for the wrap party. The shortest distance between two points being a straight line, Bud put the saddle on the pony and just walked through the lobby of the Holiday Inn. And through the main dining room passed astonished guests, up about five steps into the Convention Room, through the cast, crew and friends enjoying presentations being made by Dick Clark, to the stage at the far end of the Convention Room. He handed the lead rope of the saddled pony to Dick Clark who, in turn, presented it to the very happy and excited young lad. The wrap party for, "Killers Three" was a big success thanks again, in part, to "the Cardos way"!

Some of you know the life of a star like Dick Clark is practically devoid of privacy. Bud had a solution that would achieve the goal of anonymity for Dick so the two guys could have an evening to themselves without people pestering for autographs and have their picture taken with the world famous TV and movie star.

Bud disguised him: A floppy hat, western clothes along with the mustache Dick had already grown for his part in, "Killers Three." They made their way to a Honky-Tonk Bar, having drinks and listening to a Hill Billy Band. Dick thoroughly enjoyed himself as did his buddy, Cowboy Bud. It was another time treasured by now both close friends.

The Dick Clark Production Company returned to Hollywood. Bud stayed behind with his crew (Rick Jackson, Sue 'Huck' Arnold, and Forest Carpenter) to close all final arrangements with the town, its Mayor and all the people who helped with the production. Saying goodbye to 'Huck' and Forest; Bud and Rick headed for California in Bud's plane.

Shortly after returning home, Bud got a call from Dick Clark. In the post-production editing of the movie, the editors found that some much needed footage was missing and pick-up shots required. Dick was never pleased with the Director's work so he approached Bud for help. After seeing what was needed, Bud told Dick all the needed pick-up shots could be filmed in his old stomping grounds of Big Bear, CA. Dick hired him for the work and after doing a week's preparation painting cars and getting ready for the shoot, Bud took a small production crew to Big Bear and directed all the necessary scenes needed to complete, "Killers Three." Back in Hollywood after screening Bud's work, Dick made the comment, "I wish you had directed the whole picture for me."

A meeting at American International Pictures after viewing the finished movie, Dick was being highly complemented by Sam Arcoff and Jim Nickelson, the owners and their management level personnel complementing Dick on not only the quality of the finished product but the fact the he brought it in under budget. Dick made a statement that got back to Bud, "I could not have done it without Bud Cardos."

The Cardos baby girl was born. They named her Tammy. At her baptism in the neighborhood Catholic Church, Bud asked Dick Clark to be her God-father which he gladly accepted feeling proud to be asked by the Cardos family. Their relationship had developed where Dick had been accepted as a member of the family. Even when Bud would call his office in Hollywood to ask a question about nothing too important, he would momentarily get a call-back from Dick in Europe or wherever he was in the world.

Late one evening, Dick and his wife stopped by the Cardos home in Reseda, CA, for a visit. The ladies, Pat with baby Tammy and Dick's wife (at the time) settled in the kitchen for a 'gab fest' and the guys went into the living room with a couple of drinks. Bud noticed his friend seemed somewhat preoccupied so he asked Dick what was on his mind. Dick straightened up and came right out with it, "My wife and I are having trouble. We may not make it. I have an idea that may help us. It is a life-test, unorthodox and unusual at best. We would like to borrow your baby."

Bud just looked at his friend for a long moment and then said, "Let's go into the kitchen and talk with Pat." They did and sometime later the unusual arrangement was agreed upon by Bud and Pat. Tammy would live with the Clarks for an indefinite period of time, before having their own children. The Cardos family could visit as often as they wished. Tammy left that day with the clothes on her back and extra diapers. Dick just about emptied out the baby department of a local department store near where he lived in Studio City, CA.

Time passed and the experiment didn't work. It seems the differences between Dick and his wife just could not be resolved and having a baby in their lives did not bring the healing hoped for. Tammy was returned to the Cardos residence and the arms of Mom and Dad. Recalling that time in his life Bud admits it took a lot of convincing to get Pat to agree to the test for his friend's sake. "We visited Tammy just about every day."

Cowboy Bud took a business trip and flew his plane to Mexico scouting locations for an intended movie production with his friends, TV Star Roberto Contrasas and production manager, Dick Dixon. After achieving the intended objectives and completing the necessary arrangements in that phase of pre-production for a co-production between a Hollywood production company and Mexico, costs and union requirements, the threesome headed for home.

On the return trip Bud decided to take a break and land in Palm Springs to break up the trip. He was tired and needed rest but the tower in Palm Springs waved him off due to strong winds and bad weather. He tried Ontario, CA, and essentially got the same report. He landed at Burbank Airport and let his buddies Dick Dixon and Roberto' off. Burbank is so close to Van Nuys, Bud decided to take the last hop.

Landing at the Van Nuys Airport, Bud taxied the plane to the tie-down place assigned to him. Being late at night, he was surprised to see his fellow pilot and long-time friend, Skipper, sitting in his pick-up truck. He helped Bud tie down the plane and then gave Bud the tragic news that his daughter had drowned in his pool. It wasn't until sometime later Bud learned that his friend, Skipper out of kindness and concern, had contacted both the Palm Springs Tower and Ontario Tower and told them of the tragedy in the Cardos Family and to ward off Bud's attempt to land, in effect, to 'herd' him home.

As it is with the kind of tragedy that took little Tammy's life, it happened so fast. Pat and a girlfriend were sitting out by the pool with the child. The phone rang just as the girl went inside to the ladies room. It is just a guess but apparently Pat did not notice the girl's departure as she went to answer the phone. Tammy was left unattended just long enough for her to fall into the pool and drown. Out of consideration for Pat, Bud never questioned her about the incident. He dealt with the fact that Tammy was gone and proceeded to make funeral arrangements with his Church.

Dick Clark was as devastated as the Cardos family. At the funeral for Tammy he sat in the back of the Chapel deep in sorrow. He had bonded with the child like she was his own. The honor of being asked to be Tammy's God-father he had taken deep in his heart. As sad as the loss of Tammy was, it had a way of strengthening the Cardos-Clark bond beyond the material vanities of earthly life — a bond beyond our box of space and time.

Knowing the truth of 'activity is life and inactivity is death', Dick hired Bud to work in his current movie project entitled, "The Dark." Bud's title was Associate Producer, mainly just a title. Truthfully it should have been, 'Clark's Cop'. The director, Toby Hooper, who had directed, "The Chain Saw Murders," soon showed after a few days of principle photography that he could not stick to a budget. Even though it cost sixty-thousand dollars to Dick's production company due to a Director's Guild ruling regarding an established director's work, he hired Bud to finish directing the movie.

"The Dark" Starring: William Devane, Cathy Lee Crosby and Richard Jaeckel, has the story line set in Los Angeles where a seven-foot alien decapitates its victims and shoots laser beams from its eyes. William Devane is the father of its first victim, and teams up with a TV reporter, a rival detective and a psychic to track "The Mangler" down before it claims its next victim. The movie received less than high marks with critics but 'Sci-Fi' audiences enjoyed it.

Another Clark 'shoot' with Bud was, "The Werewolf of Woodstock," a TV movie of the week. This time Dick appealed to the actor side of Cowboy Bud and asked him to play the werewolf. Bud agreed knowing from previous experience it would mean many hours in make-up. In fact every day Bud worked on the movie he would report to the MGM Make-up Department at 3:00 am., to put on his werewolf make-up and be ready to work in front of the camera by 7:00 am. The effect on screen was memorable and a big success. Bud's physical prowess enabled him to do stunts like run up two flights of stairs carrying a girl.

Reflecting back on his life with Dick, he recalls Dick's production office on the Sunset Strip in Hollywood had a series of ten desks that led up to Dick's personal office. He couldn't help notice over a period of time that one of the secretaries kept moving closer to the boss's office, one desk at a time. Each visit the young lady had moved one desk closer to the boss. You guessed it, soon after Dick's divorce from his wife, the young lady, Kari, was seen at the desk closest to the boss's office. Not too long afterward, she became known as Mrs. Clark, married 7/7/77 for luck! To this day Bud remains in constant touch with Kari who has remained the love of Dick's life.

Bud's 'Key Art' produced in his garage, is an added facet to his talent and what he created for Dick Clark is worth mentioning because of the way it was received. Made totally from over three hundred keys, Bud created the complete stage setting of Dick's American Bandstand including every detail like the microphone, the musical instruments, music stands, musicians, lights, cameras, crew and the 'AB' for American Bandstand on the wall behind the set. When Bud presented it to Dick he was deeply moved. He placed the art work on the mantel in his office with a photograph above it of his first American Bandstand TV Show broadcast from Philadelphia, PA.

Bud and his key art

When trying to explain a man's love for his fellow man beyond the worldly yardsticks such as the applause, approval and all the material success, it is the love in our hearts for a good, moral man that created an ongoing service to his fellow man through entertainment and his multi-faceted talent. To Cowboy Bud it was the many times they just shared life together. Having a drink or sharing hot-dogs at some stand somewhere. The sadness of loss or the accolades of success, they were simply good friends. "In all of my life, Dick was one of my best friends for forty-four years. I deeply miss him." It was a form of unconditional love rarely found between men.

Dick Clark

Born: November 30, 1929, New York, NY

Died: April 18, 2012, Santa Monica, CA

Chapter Fourteen
Red, White and Black

Bud's work as an animal wrangler, stuntman, actor, set designer, unit production manager and associate producer not only for Dick Clark Productions but other independent producers like, Al Adamson, Rex Carlton and Arch Hall in such diverse movies as, "Five Bloody Graves," "Blood of Dracula's Castle," "Satan's Sadists" and "Hell's Bloody Devils" to mention a few. When he was not working in the movie business he always stayed busy as a carpenter doing construction work. His present family had grown to two girls and his son, John, Jr. And remember, there were two daughters from his first marriage to Barbara. Living expenses were really high for Dad Cardos.

Whatever the job, Bud always gave his best. When he worked as a Unit Production Manager, part of his duties were to make sure the production company was in good standing with the Screen Actors Guild. That included making sure all monies to cover the actors' salaries were in a trust account before principle photography. In an independent production away from the major studios of Hollywood, a producer does not have to sign an agreement with the labor unions for his crew but he must sign with SAG to use any of their actors. Both the producer and the actors are in severe trouble if they violate the producer's agreement with the Screen Actors Guild. The actors are subject to a heavy fine and six month suspension for working for a producer who is not a signatory of the Guild. Basically, they simply will not work for a producer who has not signed with SAG. And that is just about every actor in Hollywood of any merit.

Phil Dezen was the Actor's Representative for SAG. Bud as Unit Production Manger always made sure Phil's needs were covered and met. He never allowed any problems to arise with the actors and SAG, for their protection and that of production company. There are many rules governing movies made in Hollywood and one made on location elsewhere; mode of travel, working hours, accommodations and on and on. Bud knew them all and made sure rules were not broken. A good bond of friendship and respect developed between Bud and Phil Dezen through the years.

One day Bud got a call from Phil to come to his office for a consultation about a production that was in trouble. When Bud got to Phil's office at SAG, he met a man, Stu Hirshman, a producer in need of help. Phil asked Bud if he would look at the incomplete movie entitled, "Red, White and Black." He was told there already was seven hours of film back in Kansas where Mr. Hirshman has his company, Northern Productions.

Bud agreed to take a trip back to Kansas to view the footage. The first problem was the footage was all in sixteen millimeter film. That meant blowing the film up to thirty-five millimeter for release to the theaters. This process tends to make the finished product 'soft' or a little fuzzy. Attention to the period dress, for example was non-existent. Girls were wearing Capri pants in a story taking place in the 1800's! In fact, Bud found none of the footage usable. Long story short, it was a mess!

When Bud got back to Phil in Hollywood he told him, "Phil — they have nothing." He made an offer to go home and work on a budget to make the movie. He did and came back and told Phil he could complete the movie with his budget but only if he was the Director. He left the men to consult with each other and Stu's investors who already had $35,000 invested in, "Red, White and Black."

The word came back that Northern Productions accepted Bud's deal and he was hired as Director. In pre-production Bud worked out his shooting schedule, desired locations and started putting his cast and crew together. For Stars he contracted Caesar Romero, Barbara Hale, Robert DoQui, Rafer Johnson — Decathlon Champion in the 1960 Olympics in Rome and became a personal friend of President Kennedy — Isabelle Sanford, Janee Michelle as the leading lady and a full supporting cast. I played the Indian Chief, Walking Horse.

Caesar Ramero, Barbara Hale and Bud in Red, White and Black

The story was about black troopers who fought and killed the red man for a white government that didn't give a damn about either one! The friendship between Walking Horse and Pvt. Armstrong, played by Rafer Johnson, was an added dimension underscoring no color line between men.

Bud, 'Huck', Bob Dix as Walking Horse and Rafer Johnson as Pvt. Armstrong

Some of the principle photography was in Corriganville in CA and the balance in Ft. Davis, Texas. Bud got some odd people on the transportation end. One guy was from the Spawn Ranch where Charlie Mason had his gang of killers. For expenses and a few bucks, the guy drove the truck to Texas, then collected his pay and disappeared. It became known that Charlie did not want people leaving and there were a lot of graves to support his rule. The cowboy truck driver just wanted to escape 'The Manson Family' with his life!

When Bud shot a scene between Walking Horse and Pvt. Armstrong in Corriganville, my horse in the movie was established in the first sequence of Walking Horse's Camp where Rafer and I play a drinking scene between friends in my tee-pee. I mention this because of the horse, an appaloosa spotted gelding, I knew I would have to ride bareback in a battle sequence later in the movie. And once an animal is 'established' in a movie, it has to be the same Walking Horse's horse for the rest of the show. My horse, I affectionately called, 'Knot-head,' was trailered to Texas. How he got his name will come a little later.

Bud arranged a private DC-3 airplane for transport from CA to TX for most of the cast and crew. I kissed my wife and son goodbye and got on board with everyone else. Other members of the cast Bud flew in his 182 Cessna. We landed in Marfa, TX not far from Ft. Davis.

I and other cast members (except for the stars) were billeted in a bunk house in the Fort complex. After I threw my gear on one of the bunks, I went back out to look around. There were two corrals in the center of the fort. All the horses to be used in the movie were in one corral — except for one horse, my horse, alone in the other corral. A little concerned, I walked down to a wrangler nearby and asked him, "Why is he by himself?" The cowboy told me, "He doesn't get along well with other horses." Wondering I asked him, "Do you know if he is gun-shy?" The cowboy said, "I don't know."

Knowing I had to fire a rifle while riding my horse at a full gallop in a battle charge, I went and found the property master and checked out two Colt 44s, loaded them with full-load blanks and made my way to my horse's corral, stepped inside, closed the gate and started talking sweet talk to him. I patted his neck, let him smell the gun and putting one behind my back, fired a round. The horse jumped about four feet in the air!

I told the wrangler to please spend some time firing both pistol and rifle around him as often as possible during the total time of the production. He promised he would.

On another occasion my horse was tied to a small tree waiting for us to be called to work. For no apparent reason he suddenly started to pull on the lead rope, pulled the tree out of the ground and at a dead run headed back to the barn. I went and got him trying not to hold up the production company while they wait for Walking Horse. From that day on my horse's name was, 'Knot-head'!

Caesar Romero was a delightful man, always willing to greet fans who easily recognized him not only for his star status but his pure white hair that could be seen a long ways off. We were on a break from filming. Caesar was in his chair next to me while we both enjoyed some sun outside his room. A road passed about fifty yards in front of us. Local traffic was light. Suddenly there was a scream! A lady had slammed on her brakes, waving frantically and yelling, "Caesar Romero!" Caesar waved back just as another car rear-ended the lady's car and then another and another. Four cars with smashed headlights and taillights lined the road in front of us. The very friendly Caesar suggested we go inside for a drink. And we did.

Another humorous antidote about Caesar was one morning in his room while Bud and Caesar were talking about the shooting schedule for the day; Caesar was in the process of getting dressed. Wearing only his shorts, there was a light knock on the door followed immediately by a woman neither of the men had seen before who just let herself in to Mr. Romero's room, an exuberant fan bubbling over with admiration for the man almost totally naked in front of her. Caesar was Mr. Cool, welcomed her into his quarters and simply continued to get dressed. Bud sat in amazement at the kindness and consideration of Mr. Romero. Most stars would have thrown a fit.

It is important to note that with Cowboy Bud's first directorial assignment he wanted to pay tribute to the friendship of co-workers in the movie industry through the years both in his casting of the movie and the crew. He had not worked with Caesar Romero before but after, "Red, White and Black," they remained close friends for many years.

As mentioned in an earlier chapter, the Cardos home in Reseda, California, was always a buzz of activity on the 4th of July. Every year Caesar would show up in his "Joker" make-up giving the kids a thrill with his Joker-crazed laugh while handing out sparklers. They loved him.

Barbara Hale, also a fine actor, played the wife of the Commandant of Ft. Davis (Caesar Romero). I was cast as Walking Horse, the Indian chief. As you know, Bud and I have been close friends since the middle 1960s. Another close friend and fine actor, Steve Drexel, was cast as Captain Louis Carpenter. Steve was a special friend to Bud and me and many Hollywood singers, actors, and entertainers. We often congregated at his family owned and operated Italian restaurant, Panza's Lazy Susan, where you might see Frank Sinatra, singer/entertainer Eartha Kitt, movie star Hedy Lamar, Harry Gardino, and many others.

Bud, Rafer Johnson and Steve Drexel

One evening after work, Bud and I stopped in Panza's for a drink, sat at the bar as we usually did and after ordering our drinks from the bartender, Uncle Joe — Steve's uncle — we asked about any 'finger food'. Having nothing at the time, Bud and I came up with a 'gag'; one of us (I can't remember which one) called Pizza Hut and ordered a pizza delivered to Bud and Bob at the bar. We gave the address of Panza's without mentioning it was a restaurant.

When the delivery guy came in with that large pizza asking for Bud and Bob at the bar, the place erupted in laughter! We paid the delivery guy and he left. Needless to say, Uncle Joe, Steve, Pop and Mom Carngie (Steve's family name) were miffed but soon enjoyed the joke along with the rest of us.

Stuntman/Actor Bobby Clark as Kayitah, a longtime friend, having worked in many movies with Cowboy Bud, trailered his falling horse to Ft. Davis, Texas and Byrd Holland, character actor and make-up artist was cast as, The Sulter. Bud's eighteen month old son, 'Jon-Jon' made his debut as an Indian child. A full supporting cast of actors playing Indians, soldiers and frontier people of the early, American West.

Jon-Jon as Indian child

Sue 'Huck' Arnold was the Script Supervisor after coming to Hollywood from her work with Bud on, "Killers Three," and established herself in the Independent Production Business with Al Adamson on "Satan Sadists" and other independent productions; long time, highly qualified, legally trained and well known and close friend, Richard Dixon, as the First Assistant Director, and other men and women Bud had worked with through the years as Camera Crew, Lighting Director, make-up and all the various production departments including dear friends Bob Dietz on sound and his wife, Hedy, taking production 'stills' (photographs). Ron Coe, close friend and all around worker with Bud from stunts to hauling cable and setting lights was always part of Bud's crew.

The lead black actor playing Eli Brown, Robert DoQui, secured his wife, Janee Michelle, as the young leading lady playing Julie Brown. On her first day on the set, she kept Caesar Romero, the cast and crew waiting for five hours while she messed with her hair, make-up and wardrobe. Bud sent her husband, DoQui, to speak to her. No luck. Then he started the 'good guy – bad guy' routine with First Assistant Director, Dixon, reprimanding him for being rude to his 'star', a game often used to keep Director Cardos in a positive light. All took turns trying to get her to report to the set.

You can imagine how the spirit of both cast and crew dampened waiting for Janee. And Director Cardos on the first day of principle photography had to force himself to be the diplomat. The work finally was completed but Janee's behavior was not forgotten. To teach the young neophyte a lesson for days to come Bud put her on the call-sheet. He would keep her sitting on a hill out on location. She would never get a call to work, just sit and wait. In Texas after three days of Janee sitting around waiting to be called to work, Robert DoQui, fully aware of what Bud was doing, asked him to 'let up' on Janee. Bud agreed that maybe she had learned her lesson. Time would tell. And she was a good girl from then on.

Working with a cast that was made up of mostly black actors playing soldiers, being a diplomat became a large part of Director Bud's challenge. It was the time when a great deal of attention was being given to blacks in America, their history and suffering. As far as people in show business are concerned, if you are a performer, then perform. No one cares what the color of your skin may be, just perform or get off the stage. As the old joke in "show-biz" goes, "Or get on the next stage out of town!"

There are always crusaders who magnify America's problems. Bud had such a guy playing the part of Sargent in charge of the troops. A good actor who had a speech to a squad of the Buffalo soldiers about their duties and objectives as black American soldiers. The actor rewrote the speech to include zingers and rants underlying the black man's plight in America. He approached his boss, the artistic director of the movie and told Bud he wanted his speech modified. He read his rewrite to Bud who immediately saw what the guy was trying to do. He made a deal with the actor, "Do it as in the screenplay and then we'll do your version in a separate 'take'." The actor agreed. They did the speech twice. For the second time, the actor's version, Bud spent two hours shooting the scene from different angles with lots of close-ups on the Sargent who was well pleased with his political rant. There was no film in the camera. Don't mess with Cowboy Bud. He achieved what was needed, a happy actor and a unified cast and crew.

The completed motion picture, "Red, White and Black," was released under the title of "Soul Soldiers." The reason for the title change has already been mentioned above. It was more politically correct for the day and by the way, for its world premiere in Canada by Dimension Films, it was very well received and made its negative cost back. Producer Stu Hirshman and his partners in Northern Productions were well pleased with the finished product and their Director, John 'Bud' Cardos.

An interesting connection for Bud came in the post-production editorial work of this movie. The initial editor was having personal problems so Bud moved the work to the offices and cutting rooms of Igo Kantor. Through their work on the post-production of Bud's movie, Igo recognized the Cardos talent and immediately hired him to be his Unit Production Manager and Assistant Director on his forthcoming movie, "Judd." It was the first of many the men did together as a Producer/Director team in the years ahead.

It was a gala night for the Cardos family at the Henry Fonda Theater in Hollywood for the U. S. Premiere of "Soul Solider." Even little 'Jon-Jon' was in a tuxedo with Mom Pat and Dad Bud in their finest evening gown and tuxedo. Search lights scanning the heavens, camera's flashing, movie stars and the long, black limousines, TV cameras and hundreds of people all there to see Cowboy Bud's first directorial bid. Rousing applause and whistles and cheers erupted at the conclusion of the screening, a very special memory in the career of Director, John 'Bud' Cardos.

Premier of "Red, White and Black" in front of theater

While in production in Texas, Stu Herishman, the producer, would fly into Marfa, Texas where Bud would meet him and then fly him in his plane to Ft. Davis, a short hop, where the principle photography was taking place on, "Red, White and Black." On one such weekend,

Bud offered to fly Stu and Caesar Romero to Mexico for lunch in the town of Ojioga on the Mexican side of the International Border. They accepted and the trio took off in Bud's plane. The learned procedure on such a trip was Bud would land his plane on the U.S. side of the border on a dirt strip, walk across the border and avoid the lengthy inspection when landing in Mexico.

It was late morning when the men got to the local restaurant for lunch. A main room featured a table in the center surrounded by tables on the fringe of the main room. The management immediately recognized Caesar Romero and seated the men at the center table. Still being early for the lunch hour, they were the only customers. As luck would have it, Caesar forgot his glasses and he was the most bilingual man present. Stu started trying to communicate with the waiter using sounds that he thought helped clarify the menu. It became a very funny scene as people started to enter the dining area, spotted the world famous movie star, Caesar Romero with his American friends with Stu's voice getting louder as he tried to phonetically decipher the menu. It was good fun while Caesar met and greeted local fans.

After lunch on a walk through the little town there was an enthusiastic group of people following the good natured Caesar, Stu and Bud. When the time came to depart for the U.S., fond farewells followed the men up to the border. The trip was a good break from the intense life of making a movie with a cast and crew of over a hundred people.

An added and big plus for "Red, White and Black" aka "Soul Soldier," were the five paintings created from scenes in the movie by the renowned painter, A. Kelly Pruitt, and were used as backdrops for the main titles of the movie. It gave the impression of a top of the line, big budget and major-studio effect. They are beautiful paintings.

A. Kelly Pruitt painting

Chapter Fifteen
The Dark

By now good friend and Producer, Dick Clark, along with producer, Ed Montoro, a movie was slated for production under the title of "The Dark." Bud was hired as the Line Producer but more like the eyes and ears of his friend, Dick Clark. Clark wanted Bud to direct but co-producer Montoro wanted Director, Tobe Hooper, for the show because he did such a masterful job with, "The Texas Chain Saw Massacre."

What they did not take into consideration was that Director Hooper did not have a time limitation with, "Chainsaw" which was two years in the making with a Skelton Crew of about eight people working on weekends and holidays. Shooting to a budget with a crew of over eighty people was overwhelming. After three days of filming, Hooper was already a week behind on the shooting schedule. The producers stepped in and replaced him with Bud. One of the stars, William Devane, was upset with the change in directors but soon accepted Director Cardos. In fact, it was Bud that helped Tobe Hooper become a member of the Directors Guild of America.

The storyline: Los Angeles is being stalked by a seven-foot alien that decapitates its victims and shoots laser beams from its eyes. William Devane is the father of its first victim, and teams up with a TV reporter, a rival detective and a psychic to track "The Mangler" down before it claims its next victim. A line associated with the marketing of the movie was, "You don't have to be afraid of the dark — just what is in it!"

The cast also starred, Richard Jaeckel, who became one of Bud's closest friends away from their work in movies. I met him one afternoon at the Cardos poolside where many of Bud's friends would enjoy time in the sun. Nice man — a very down to earth kind of guy. The female lead in the part of Zoe Owens, was played nicely by Cathy Lee Crosby and radio star Casey Kasem, did well in the role of the Police Pathologist. The seven-foot, two-inch John Bloom did a masterful job as, "The Mangler." Keenan Wynn and other fine actors are part of the supporting cast along with Jay Lawrence, Country Western Radio DJ in L.A., Bud cast as one of the cops as he had also done in, "Kingdom of the Spiders." The thanks was Jay gave a running commentary on the air while Director Cardos worked on, "The Dark."

Keenan Wynn, Cathy Lee Crosby and Bud

Bud had a growing reputation for his work stemming from the "Kingdom" success. In the independent film business a director that brings a movie in at budget or under budget is highly valued. Director Cardos was always able to achieve this goal and maintain artist quality.

Another example of the Cardos ingenuity was "The Dark" story called for a sports car driven throughout the story by actor William Devane. Bud sent a transportation driver to Detroit where he met Bud's cousin who had lined up a 'demo' Corvette for $8,000. Bud paid for the car with his own funds and the driver drove it to California. Then Cowboy Bud rented the Corvette to the production company. A police radio was installed for the story point of Devane listening in and following police calls in pursuit of, The Mangler. By the end of production the car rental repaid Bud's cost of the car.

About this time a man that many production people in Hollywood knew, Ray Dorn, owner of the Hollywood Studio on Santa Monica Blvd, was also a builder of sets. In a sequence where a stewardess is walking in a darkened car-park underground, Ray built a wall made out of Styrofoam that looked like a solid wall. At the right moment, The Mangler, threw a body through the wall accompanied by the shrieks and screams of the stewardess. A dramatic high point along with others created.

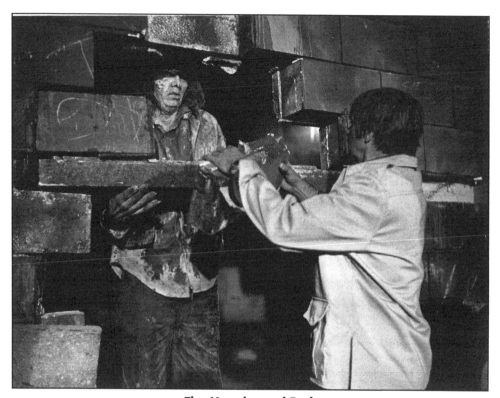

The Mangler and Bud

Ray was one of those characters always seen wearing a blue pair of overalls. That was it, day in and day out with a can of beer in each front pocket. We all liked him. He wanted to learn how to fly so Bud taught him over time. Then he asked Bud to buy his Tri-Pacer Airplane. Bud gave him a good price. Ray bought the plane and flew it out to his ranch where some time later on a visit, Bud saw what was left of his plane. Maybe it was one too many beers but the plane that Bud had babied and kept in pristine condition looked like it had been pulled through a hedge backwards! It was heartbreak for Cowboy Bud who kept all his rolling stock like new including his location truck, a 1957 panel truck he inherited when his dear friend and co-worker, Forrest Carpenter, passed on.

Striving to always get the best, Director Bud put on his 'stunt hat' and with fellow stuntman, McCarthy, his wild Irish friend, they performed a car stunt. The stunt was designed to have two cars racing toward each other at a high speed coming close but not colliding. The two guys drove speeding at each other coming so close they knocked the rear vision mirrors off both cars, a very dangerous and potentially fatal 'car gag' in the lingo of stuntmen.

"The Dark" had a good run with audiences who enjoyed horror movies. Director Cardos was able to bring the production in on budget. It still can be purchased through Amazon. com on DVD.

Chapter Sixteen
Mutant aka Night Shadows

Want to be scared? Director Cowboy Bud Cardos was given another challenge in the frightening story called, "Mutant," that was released under the title of "Night Shadows," co-produced by Dick Clark. History repeats itself when co-producer, Ed Montoro, called Bud to the rescue as Director. Again, the same problem of the initial Director, a young hopeful who had written the screenplay, Mark Rosman, was hired by Ed to direct. Fortunately, for the producers they had hired Bud as the Line Producer and Unit Production Manager.

In a week of preparation in Hollywood, Bud got familiar with the script, helped with the casting of the various parts in the story (Bo Hopkins as the sheriff) and other cast members, Wings Hauser in the lead role and Jennifer Warren to play the veterinarian. Jody Medford cast in the role of Holly Pierce along with a full supporting cast. Some from Hollywood and others cast locally in Atlanta, GA.

Mutant — Wings Hauser and Jody Medford

The locations were in and around Atlanta, GA. In advance of the arrival of the full crew, Mark Rosman picked out locations for the principle photography for the story. Not being a knowledgeable film director many were not the best for filming with a full crew. And he was unable to stick to a shooting schedule. In the first few days of shooting he was running over budget.

When this type of crisis happens the panic button is pushed. By the time the decision was made to replace Rosman and hire Bud he had little time to approach the story as a director. Producer Ed Montoro gave him a Friday off and the balance of a weekend to be ready to take over the following Monday morning. Bud had to prepare for production. Planning his shooting schedule and the many aspects of preparation to direct a motion picture, include the coordination of lighting, sound, guidance for each actor and the character he or she is portraying and mapping out scene coverage for the camera — are just a few of the responsibilities of a Director in Hollywood. You are usually judged by your last movie so your reputation is on the line. Preparing for principle photography in a weekend is a big challenge!

The story line of "Mutant," goes, in brief, as follows. Two brothers discover that the residents of a small Southern town are being infected by a form of toxic waste, turning them into blood-ravenous zombies.

On every movie there are some funny or exasperating moments. One on "Mutant" for Director Bud was when the actress, Jody Medford playing Holly Pierce, came to him and said, "I cain't do it!" The scene followed a roll over car-crash where Jody was to exit from the wrecked car and crawl over the wreckage to safety.

Director Bud, naturally a little upset with the actress, asked her, "Why can't you do this scene?" Confidentially Jody said to her Director, "I don't have any panties on." As the camera angles had been mapped out by Bud, there was no way for him to shoot the scene without panties on Jody. The whole production company had to shut down while Enid, Igo Kantor's wife and a secretary rushed to the nearest town and got Jody a pair of panties. The effort was further marred by the fact the company was shooting "night for night," just one of the unforeseen production problems that pop up.

Another incident that blind-sided Bud was producer Ed coming up to him with some shocking news about Enid Kantor, Igo Kantor's wife who was working with the production staff, "Enid is in jail!" Apparently, she had broken a local traffic law and with the smell of alcohol on her breath, the local cop not knowing or believing she was with the Hollywood Production Company making a movie, took her directly to jail. Being more embarrassing than anything else, it was all worked out with a necessary fine being paid.

Wings, Bud and Igor Kantor

Producer Ed Montoro came to Bud at the Wrap Party of the movie and said to him, "Bud — you saved my ass." The credit as Director of "Mutant" aka "Night Shadows," further advanced John Bud Cardos as a Director who could bring in a production on time and on budget giving the producer the best "bang for the buck." His reputation remained solid in the Hollywood community.

As a little unknown Hollywood history that now can be told, Producer Ed Montoro and his wife ended their marriage with a terrible argument. It was believed by insiders, that was why Ed cleaned out his bank accounts of several million dollars and was last seen heading toward Mexico in his motor home never to be heard of again. Is he still there? God only knows.

Chapter Seventeen
The Day Time Ended

One of Cowboy Bud's closest friends was the Actor Jim Davis. In "The Day Time Ended" the men had another opportunity to work together. Director Cardos had gained a reputation with other independent production companies, as mentioned, for bringing "A" class actors like Jim Davis to the lower budget movies. In this Sci-Fri story he also was able to cast Chris Mitchum; the wonderful actress Dorothy Malone, and among other qualified actors, another of Bud's long-time friends, Roberto Contreas from the popular TV series "High Chaparral."

The story follows a small family as it relocates to the Sonoran Desert, to be closer to the grandparents of the family. Though there are news reports of a spectacular triple supernova, and the young granddaughter has seen a glowing alien construction behind the barn, the family is at ease until, one night, a UFO soars overhead and appears to land in the nearby hills.

Apparently, the triple supernova has opened a rift in space and time. The family finds that their electrical appliances no longer function, and the youngest daughter of the family has a telepathic encounter with an extra-terrestrial. The grandmother, too, sees one of these diminutive creatures beckoning to her, but it soon vanishes.

The grandfather, while trying to start the car, sees that a strange animal is approaching from the distance. He goes back inside and informs the family that something is coming; before long, a variety of horrific, alien monsters (all of these creatures being of a reptilian or amphibious nature) are proceeding to slaughter each other outside the house; some are trying to break in and kill the family. After a few moments, the same UFO from before appears in the sky, and teleports the creatures to a different place.

The family takes this opportunity to escape to the barn, which is more easily defensible than the house. They become separated from one another and each hides until sunrise, where they find that they have been launched thousands of years into the future.

They meet up with the daughter, who had become separated from the family during one of the time-warp events. She knows, somehow, that everything is going to be fine now. After walking across the desert, they finally see a doomed city in the distance, and decide to seek refuge there. The grandfather (Jim Davis) proclaims that there must be a purpose to all of this to be discovered one day. The family walks off into the distance, having survived, "The Day Time Ended."

Cowboy Bud and Jim had fun creating as many scary moments in the movie and Bud says he doesn't mind if someone buys a bag of popcorn, he just doesn't want them to eat it.

Not every movie is a wonderful experience. Producer Charles Band left Bud hanging with promises never fulfilled. Fortunately for Jim Davis' friendship with Bud that kept him on the job. Therefore although "The Day Time Ended" did reasonable well in the market it is not a happy memory.

The highlights of the production were the lasting friendship between Bud and Chris Mitchum. When the work was done, Cowboy Bud, Jim and Chris toasted drinks to the end of "The Day Time Ended."

Chapter Eighteen
Drag Racer

To quote a description of Cowboy Bud Cardos from a reviewer on the Internet, "Versatile and underrated B-Movie renaissance man, John Bud Cardos..." gives insight to Bud's reputation as a Director and all around movie-man. The variety of stories captured on film by him is further illustrated by a very rare and seldom seen youth-oriented racing movie. It is the story of a young man's dream to get a ride in a top fuel dragster, a very different story line from Director Bud's usual action assignments.

He was visiting his producer friend, Igo Kantor at Igo's post production facility in Hollywood where he met Robert Glenn. Mr. Glenn immediately engaged Bud in conversation about his original screenplay, Drag Racer. He knew of Director Bud from seeing his movies and the fine and friendly introduction he received from Igo Kantor with reports of the projects he and Bud had worked on in the recent past. The Glenn Production Company with the added asset of Glenn's brother, a champion drag racer as technical advisor, hired Director John Bud Cardos on the spot.

Bud at the Irwindale Raceway

At this time in Bud's career he was flying a Cessna 182 airplane so he would fly over the L.A. traffic and land his plane on one of the several drag strips and race tracks in Southern California and a more distant location in Amarillo, Texas. Bud recalls, "Having my plane near my house at the Van Nuys Airport allowed many advantages including saving time by flying over commuter traffic on the freeways."

Bud helped Robert Glenn with the casting of the leads and supporting players. The main leads were John Chandler as 'Dave', a tall and thin man with fair hair, piercing blue eyes, a pale complexion and a nasal, whiny voice Bud had worked with in Canada. Chandler specialized in portraying mean, neurotic and dangerous villains. He made an impressive film debut in his sole starring part as the titular sniveling, psychotic, homicidal weasel gangster in, "Mad Dog Coll."

The other younger, starring roles were, Deborah Walley of "Gigget" fame in the leading role along with Jeremey Slate as, "Ron," you have seen Jeremy Slate in many roles since both on TV and in motion pictures, a fine actor in both comedy and dramatic roles. Mark Slade co-starred as "Jeff," Karen Swanson as "Julie," and Preston Pierce as "Norm." "Sheila" was played by Kitty Murray and "Stan" by Mark Hopkins, both working actors at the time. The rest of the supporting cast filled out the balance of the actors playing the colorful characters seen around the drag strips of America.

A pleasant surprise was the visit from Cowboy Bud's good friends Jim Davis and Slim Pickens. Bud recollects Jim saying with a smile, "Sure are a lot of horses under those hoods." Slim's response with his famous chuckle, "And noises too!" They all laughed.

Jim Davis and Slim Pickens with Bud

Chapter Nineteen
The Female Bunch

The "Legends of Hollywood" is a short list. Most actors enjoy a three to five year run and then fade. One name that is on the list of legends is that of Lon Chaney, a big star in the silent movies. His son, Lon Chaney, Jr., began following in his father's footsteps in 1935 scoring his biggest success playing the part of "Lennie" in the motion picture production of Shakespeare's, "Of Mice And Men," in 1939. His sensitive and dimensional performance catapulted him to the star category as a character actor. His portrayal of "The Wolfman" in movies scared kids all over the world including me!

Director Bud connected with Lon Chaney, Jr., in the making of "The Female Bunch." The men became friends and enjoyed both a personal and professional relationship producing a successful effort in making the movie. The two men had a special bond. Bud had played the werewolf in "The Werewolf Of Woodstock" for his producer friend, Dick Clark. His make-up call was 3:00 am., at MGM Make-up department. He laughs when remembering he used to fall asleep in the make-up chair and waking up to be shocked by the image in the make-up mirror in front of him. Then he had to discover how to feed himself. At lunch time he would have to open the mouth of the werewolf mask and with chopsticks find his recessed mouth, feeding himself in small, manageable bites.

With the werewolf make-up, Bud found his intricate mask very different from Lon Chaney Jr.'s version. A pointed nose and face, cables connected to facial muscles for changing expressions. Getting something to drink was achieved through a long straw, some of the discomforts that go with being creative. Lon Chaney, Jr., was not as lucky as Bud. The make-up used for his "Wolfman" left him with facial skin sensitivity that bothered him the rest of his life.

The production of a rowdy and wild action story was nothing new for Director Bud Cardos. This effort was underscored by a particularly unique stunt done by Bud in his own plane for co-director Al Adamson; a scene that called for the actress playing "Sandy" (Nesa Renet) as a confused, wealthy girl and owner of a personal plane, to land it on a narrow dirt road and taxi up to a motel at the end of the road.

To get the needed scene on film without an editorial cut, Bud flew his plane circling the motel location and dirt road below. On cue from Director Adamson below, he descended with "Sandy" visible at the controls for the camera. Flying the plane from the opposite side away from the camera, Bud began the decent cracking the passenger door enough to see the dirt road until touchdown. He guided the plane through the crack in the door right up to the group of the girl-gang waiting in front of the motel. Bud cut the engine after breaking to a stop and "Sandy" stepped out of the plane and walked up to her new found friends. All this was done in one continuous shot from the camera car following from a three quarter shot of the approaching airplane showing "Sandy" landing the plane and joining the girls. The audience would never know the difference.

The brief story line is after a string of bad times with men, Sandy tries to kill herself. Co-waitress Libby saves her and takes her to meet some female friends of hers who live on a ranch in the desert where Lon Cheney was the foreman. Grace, the leader of the gang, puts Sandy through her initiation and they get on with the real job of running drugs across the Mexican border, hassling poor farmers, taking any man they please, and generally raising hell. Soon, Sandy becomes unsure if this is the life for her but it may be too late to get out.

The cast was enhanced by the multi-talented Russ Tamblyn playing the part of "Bill," with co-star Jennifer Bishop in the role of "Grace," who worked with Adamson in several other movies. In fact, most all of the additional cast members were actors who could be referred to as "Adamson Players;" Regina Carrol and Don Epperson being two of the prominent names.

It is good to remember in the independent motion picture production work, people often cross over depending on what is called for in the screenplay. In "The Female Bunch," Cowboy Bud also played the part of "The Mexican Farmer," which entailed Bud being hung up in a tree by barbed wire and later dragged by the cruel girl-gang across the rough terrain. The scenes were brutal on the screen. The audience never knew Cowboy Bud had clipped off the sharp points of the barbed wire.

Bud being strangled by barbed wire — The Female Bunch

He helped with all production responsibilities as the Unit Production Manager, doing stunts and working as the Second Unit Director and brought a long time horse-woman, Betsy Pallada, with an assistant, "Mike" Wendler (also a horse-woman) who taught the "gal

gang" how to ride horses and look comfortable in the saddle; not an easy job! Most actors and actresses when asked, "Can you ride?" — Usually say, "Sure," even if they don't know which end of the horse eats!

Lon Chaney, Jr, Betsy Pallada

The independent production of "The Female Bunch," was filmed entirely on location in the beautiful country of Capital Reef, Utah.

Chapter Twenty
Cowboy Bud in Africa

In the production of both TV and Feature Movies there are many independent production companies today. Up until the 1960's, the seven major studios (MGM, 20TH Century Fox, Warner Brothers, Columbia Pictures and Universal Studios and Republic and RKO) provided most all movies in the early days of Hollywood.

One of the most successful independent production companies is, Cannon Films. You may have seen their company logo at the beginning of several TV series, a piece of paper coming out of a typewriter as a logo for the company.

Harry Alan Towers of Cannon Films contacted Bud regarding a forthcoming movie, "GOR II or "Outlaw of GOR." The old story came to the fore again. A director was hired to direct a two picture deal for Cannon films. By the close of the first production, the director was already usurping funds needed for the second feature motion picture. Bud's ability to direct an action movie and bring it in on budget had become well known in Hollywood. After several meetings to discuss high points of the story, Cannon Films signed Bud to direct "GOR II," and fired the other director. "GOR II" was to be filmed entirely in Africa. Cowboy Bud took the assignment in spite of a short time to prep the show.

One of the barriers Director Bud had to overcome was with the actors playing the parts of Cabot and his midget friend. On several occasions they confronted Bud by questioning his directorial instructions. They liked the other director and naturally from the actor's point of view, they could care less about budget problems. It took time but slowly but surely, Bud won them over to his directorial moves without alienating the actors. Not an easy task. Bud always tried to promote harmony on the movie set.

He did get help from his movie star friend, Jack Palance, who was playing one of the leading roles of "Xenos" in the movie. There was a scene where one of the actors giving Bud an argument about a piece of business that called for the actor to eat a plate of food. The actor was complaining saying he did not want to eat the food offered because he felt his character would refuse it. While the camera was rolling on the scene, Jack simply took the plate of food and in one swift move plastered the plate into the face of the actor. It solved the problem. It was on film. End of discussion.

All adjustments considered including a secretary assigned to Bud that was tattooed from head to toe but ended up being very proficient and his arrival and work in Africa settled into a comfortable production with mutual respect between the cast and crew. But only Jack was invited on weekends to go on local adventures with Bud.

Obviously, from the title it is a science fiction theme. The finished product is presented to an audience interested in the imaginary world of the solar system created in the mind of a writer.

Better known as "Outlaw" to those of you who watch the TV show, "Mystery Science Theater 3000"— it is about a beefy blonde and her oily friend, Watney. They are teleported by a rose quartz to the GOR planet. "The Elder" (he has no name, just "The Elder") thinks that Xenos, a drunken priest played by Jack Palance, has eyes for the throne. Of course, Prof. Cabot cares nothing for such intrigue; just for the Princess he had "ooh-la-la" with from the previous film "GOR." The Elder is off, though. It's the Queen who wants the throne for her own. Watney is seduced by the Queen to implicate Cabot in murdering the King.

Jack Palance and Bud — Outlaw of Gor

Cabot and his platinum blonde midget friend, escape off into the desert, where they free a slave girl and are just as quickly captured by a bounty hunter. The Princess is forced by the Queen to fight, The Leather Women, a group of women who have been in the sun too long! Just kidding — I have not seen the movie.

An unforgettable experience for Cowboy Bud and his friend, movie star Jack Palance, happened off the set of "GOR II." Bud was having a drink after work at the local hotel bar when a man approached, introduced himself and explained he was the owner and operator of "Mubula," a game park preserve including thousands of acres providing protection for the African wild animals. The kind man invited Bud to see his game reserve, his hotel and cabin compound. He extended his invitation for Bud to bring his movie star friend, Jack Palance. Bud gladly accepted the invitation which opened up a memorable experience for both Jack and Bud.

Bud and Lion cub — Mubula Game Preserve

On weekends he and Jack were given safaris by the owner of the complex. In the process, a young girl, Nickki, an employee of the game park, became an avid fan and friend of the movie men to the extent that she would always insist on being their driver. A swim in a local river was one of the side pleasantries with the friendly gal. When Bud's son, John, came to Africa for a visit, he worked as a stuntman and crew member and dated Nickki for the duration of the production. Nickki became a good friend and was most helpful to her movie friends.

Friendships lasted through the production of "GOR II" and the next Cannon Film produced in the same area of Johannesburg, South Africa, "Skeleton Coast," the second Cardos directed movie; a deal consummated after Bud had returned to Hollywood about a month after completing "GOR II." Both Bud and Jack Palance have wonderful memories of the time shared at the Mubula Game Reserve along with Ernie Borgnine and other cast members from "Skeleton Coast."

One safari led by Nickki was an all day excursion into the wilds of Africa to see elephants in their natural habitat. The very disappointed Ernie and Bud returned to the Mubula Center not seeing one elephant all day. However, in the middle of that night, there was pounding on the wall between Bud's and Ernie's duplex rooms with Ernie shouting, "Bud, get up! You have got to see this."

Bud met Ernie on the porch of the duplex and there in the Mubula Complex, right before their eyes, were fifteen elephants casually eating small trees and other foliage. The men made themselves comfortable in a couple of chairs and sipping on some beers watched the scene unfolding before them. Some of the elephants were as close as ten feet from them until the herd went on its way.

In the morning Nickki arrived saying, "I found out where the elephants are. We'll find them today." Laughing and with great delight, Bud and Ernie told her of the fantastic nature show of the herd of elephants the night before.

On another safari, the group came upon an ostrich sitting on her nest of eggs. As they do, when an egg is not healthy, the ostrich kicks it out of the nest. There were three about ten feet from the nest and Bud immediately asked Nickki to stop. Both a friend, Dennis, and Bud wanted one of the eggs for a keepsake. Nickki warned them stating the ostrich would attack and they are fast on their feet. Naturally, Bud did not accept that he could not have an ostrich egg for a keepsake from Africa. He worked out a plan where Dennis would wait. Bud distracted the big bird while Dennis would run up, grab an egg and return to the safety of their vehicle. They continued their routine until the three large ostrich eggs were in their possession. According to a procedure known to Nickki, she poked a hole in each egg and proceeded to "blow the egg" to empty them. To not do this, the trophy's contents would rot in the sun making it totally undesirable as a keepsake. To this day, Bud has the ostrich egg on display in his home.

On "Skeleton Coast" a memorable evening for Cowboy Bud was the night he met, Oliver

Reed, the well-known movie star at the first company dinner with the full cast and crew before production. Reed and his wife were in attendance along with the other actors. But the occasion is remembered because of Mr. Reed. Director Bud had worked with Ernie Borgnine several times before "Skeleton" but some of the other stars he did not know personally. So the introductory dinner was designed for everybody to 'break the ice' before production began. Alcohol flowed and in a while after consuming a little more than his share, Oliver Reed announced to all the guests it was time for him to expose "his rose." With no further ado, he stood up, unzipped his pants and proudly displayed a tattooed rose on his penis. Reed was one of those personalities that could do outrages things and people just accepted his behavior.

Bud got to know Oliver Reed and his antics. After working together on the movie set for a while at a smaller, more intimate dinner party, Reed's young wife told Bud about his pride in his penis saying "He always does that." Naturally Bud asked, "Doesn't that bother you?" Oliver's wife responded, "No, that's Oliver and I love him."

Reed realized his exposing himself did not set well with Cowboy Bud, so before exposing his "rose," he would tell Bud, "I think it is time for you to leave." Happily Bud would comply. Or Oliver Reed would excuse himself and head for the "men's only bar" that existed in South Africa to share his tattoo.

Cowboy Bud always had a deep love for his children. At this point in time, he did as he always did when possible; invite his kids to join him on different movie locations. His oldest daughters, Cindy and Judy from his marriage to Barbara and his three kids from his marriage to Pat; the oldest Debbie, the second girl, Kimberly and the youngest, son John, all saw much of the world at different times in their lives.

His daughter, Debbie, then about seventeen years old, came for a visit on the "Skeleton" production, working in the wardrobe department and enjoying her trip to the continent of Africa. Part of her adventure was to go sky diving with some of her new found friends in Africa without telling her Dad knowing full well if she asked permission the answer would have been a firm "no!" She told her Dad AFTER the dive smiling with that knowing look daughters use to appease their father. What could Bud do except give her a hug and say, "I'm glad you are alright."

Son John arrived and worked again doing stunts and doubling for the actor, Ray Sharkey. Kimberly, the younger of the two daughters also came for about a two week visit. She had the life changing experience of seeing Africa and working with her Dad. John and Kimberly were both in their teens.

A culture shock for Debbie was her first lunch served in cafeteria style on the outside movie set. Native African women were employed as servers, kitchen help and crew members according to educational levels and ability. Not until that luncheon had Debbie considered native African girls and women did not use bras. It was her first experience being served lunch by servers with bare breasts. A custom she soon got used to.

A positive aspect of the "Skeleton Coast" movie was a strong cast which had been contracted to do the movie. In the starring roles were Ernie Borgnine as "Col. Bill Smith," by now a close friend of Cowboy Bud; Robert Vaughn as "Maj. Schneider," Oliver Reed as "Capt. David Simpson," Herbert Lom as "Elia" and Simone Sabela as "Sekassi" in one of the female leads. A powerful cast with big stars of the day supported by an equally strong supporting cast. The locations in Africa were also unique, colorful and expansive.

After viewing the finished movie, "Skelton Coast," the action sequences created by director Cardos are his usual excellent quality. One particular stunt involving the crash of a twin engine airplane leaves the most lasting impression. Star Ernie Borgnine gave his best to bring believability to the film's theme as did all the stars of "Skeleton Coast."

After Bud delivered the post production "Director's Cut" of "Skeleton Coast," to Harry Alan Towers of Cannon Films, he returned to his home in California with a promise from Alan Towers of a third picture in Africa.

During this break, Igo Kantor, the long-time producer friend of Bud's, called him to a meeting in Hollywood. Knowing Bud had just completed two feature films in Africa, Igo filled Bud in on a story he would like to do in Africa and Greece written by a screenwriter they both knew from former productions, Hal Reed. And he would pay twenty-five percent more than Canon had offered for Bud's services as a Director putting the offer into six figures.

The name of the project was, "Act Of Piracy." Cowboy Bud had only a verbal promise from Canon Films and they were a non-union company, whereas Kantor Productions was a union production company, offering better conditions and assurances for the Director. An added plum presented by Igo Kantor was he had secured actor, Gary Busey, to play the lead role in the story. Busey was "hot" at the time due to the box office success of his part in the movie, "Lethal Weapon," starring Mel Gibson. Busey's services would cost $500,000 but Igo thought he was worth it. Bud agreed to direct, "Act Of Piracy."

Cowboy Bud and Igo Kantor took two pre-production trips to both Africa and Greece to secure locations and reserve accommodations for the cast and crew, including finding the yacht needed for much of the story; a story about a man, Ted Andrews (Gary Busey) and his estranged wife, Sandy (played by Belinda Baur).

Busey persuades Baur to allow their two children to accompany him on his multi-million dollar yacht on a journey to Australia (where he has an offer to buy the yacht). After a few days out of port, his girlfriend, Laura (Nancy Mulford) is discovered to be a member of a terrorist organization that wants the yacht as a base of operations.

They attack and when the smoke clears, the two children are held as hostages. Busey (as Ted Andrews) manages to escape. Together with his wife, they pursue the terrorists and eventually free their children. The effort eventually brings the original family back together.

A condition of Mr. Busey's contract was he would have his own stuntman signed on for the "run of the show." Director Bud had not met Gary Busey or his stuntman so introductions did not take place until the total cast and crew got together for the production phase of the motion picture which began on the little Greek coastal town of Sykies. The hotel secured by producer Igo Kantor and Bud on their pre-production trip was not a five star hotel but clean with nice rooms as suites with living room, sitting room and bedroom.

Cowboy Bud was just getting settled into his room when he heard screaming and yelling from down the hall. Concerned, he checked it out. It was Gary Busey bitching about the size of his quarters. Not only did he demand two adjoining rooms but insisted on a king size bed. It turned out Igo Kantor had to send to Athens for the bed. This was Bud's introduction to the star of the movie he was responsible for bringing in on budget in the most harmonious way possible. Obviously, it was going to be rough going.

Busey's stuntman brought his wife along. To make a point, Bud had Jack Bower, the production manager, put the stuntman on the call sheet for every day of production although he was not needed. When the day did come for him to do a fall not over ten feet into pads and cardboard boxes (that had been tested by Bud's visiting son, John, several times and was, by all standards, an easy "gag"), he refused saying it was too dangerous. His wife even left the set completely embarrassed and left the next day for the U. S.

John Cardos, doubling as Ray Sharkey, diving off the yacht Act of Piracy

Busey developed a crush on his co-star, Belinda Baur, causing further complications. Besides showing off at every opportunity trying to "make points" with Belinda, he would also offer directions for her. Fortunately, she would agree and do just what Director Cardos wanted in a given scene.

In contrast, Actor Ray Sharkey, was a gem of a man to work with. He was always prepared to work and help in any way he could. He played the bad guy and did an excellent job. Almost in the last scene of the movie (Sharkey is being doubled by Bud's son, John), as he was pulled to his death by the sinking yacht with a rope caught around his neck.

The original family of Ted Andrews (Busey) his wife, Sandy and their children survive in a life-boat after avoiding death in the sinking of the yacht and appreciating each other in a renewed life together.

Chapter Twenty-One
Cowboy Hall of Fame

The most cherished award for any man known for his life as an American Cowboy is being honored with an invitation into the Cowboy Hall of Fame in Oklahoma. As you know, Cowboy John Bud Cardos spent many days of his youth riding, training and working with many animals, particularly with horses either on the trail, in the movies and in the Rodeo Arena clowning with his horse, "Double Trouble" known as, "DT." His horse stunts in movies are too numerous to mention both as a stuntman and Stunt Gaffer.

Igo Kantor, as you know, is an independent producer and a man who admired Bud's talent in the movie industry, and having worked together on his last movie, "Piracy." Also, knowing his background in all things Western, Igo invited Cowboy Bud to direct a docudrama entitled, "Legends of the West." It was filmed in, Tombstone, AZ, the location of the famous, "Gunfight at the OK Corral." The stars were, Jack Palance, Brooke Shields, and Jack's son who played "Billy the Kid."

Legends of the West — from left to right, Bud Cardos, Tom Daniels, Jack Palance, Igo Kantor, Dennis KC Parks and the executive producer

The second segment of "Legends" was, "Custer's Last Stand," narrated by Jack Palance and Indian Floyd "Red Cloud" Westerman. Director Cardos staged the live action battle sequences in the Custer's Monument Park in Montana that were intercut with many of the Hollywood Western Stars from studio archives. Episodes from their work in movies or TV helped to underscore the title of the series, "Legends of the West." It is sad to report that the balance of the series was never completed due to promised funding that ran into legal problems, the fate of too many Hollywood productions.

The finished product was requested by the Cowboy Hall of Fame people and behold! Cowboy Bud was invited to visit the celebration held in Oklahoma to pick up his award as Director of "Legends of the West!" A very complete itinerary of everything, from first class airfare, to a chauffeured limousine to the Cowboy Hall of Fame plus all expenses for Cowboy Bud and a guest.

A friend who Bud had mentored, Porf Dominques, in the movie business became the lucky recipient of the invitation to be Bud's companion on this most honored event. Needless to say, it was an unforgettable event in his life. He was thrilled! Porf went right out and bought a Western Tuxedo.

They flew first class to the Cowboy Hall of Fame event in Oklahoma City, OK. The plane was met by a very attractive lady attorney in her new Mercedes Benz. She was their chauffeur during the entire visit. It was an event centered on the recipients of the awards at a presentation in the main room of the Cowboy Hall of Fame. To Bud's amazement, a lady took his arm for the presentation, a world-wide Star of movies with John Wayne, Maureen O'Hara. He was in shock, flabbergasted, honored beyond words to have such a great lady on his arm. They both received their awards along with Igo Kantor as Executive Producer and Tom Daniels, Producer of "Legends of the West."

Afterwards, wherever they went up to and including the plane ride home, Porf would announce the presence of "Mr. Bud Cardos, the winner as Director of 'Legends of the West,' at the Cowboy Hall of Fame!"

With all the good memories of the daily and nightly events, one stands out in Bud's mind because of its inconsistency with the Cowboy Hall of Fame and all the Western movie stars, Bronc-busting cowboys and Rodeo Hero's honored by it plus the western history of the state of Oklahoma itself. While still in Oklahoma, a visit to Elk's Lodge (a national organization) where Bud has been a member for many, many years, he was met with the rule, "All Hats Off — Cowboys too!"

Bud and award from Cowboy Hall of Fame

Our hats off to, Cowboy 'Bud' Cardos!

– Fin –

29077562R00083

Made in the USA
Middletown, DE
07 February 2016